SRFLIS series in library science / ed. by Dr K P Singh ; no.15

Cutter-Sanborn Three-Figure Author Table Supplemented with Indian Names

Cutter-Sanborn Three-Figure Author Table Supplemented with Indian Names

M.P. Satija
Honorary Professor
Guru Nanak Dev University

Ess Ess Publications
New Delhi

Cutter-Sanborn Three-Figure Author Table Supplemented with Indian Names

Satija, M.P.
Cutter-Sanborn three-figure author table supplemented with Indian names/ M.P. Satija. — New Delhi: Ess Ess Publications, 2020.
xiii, 207 p.:Ill; 23 cm. – (SRFLIS series in library science/ed. by Dr. K P Singh; no.15).
ISBN: 978-93-87698-39-0
1. Book numbers. 2. Cutter, C.A.– Biography. 3. Shelflisting. I. Title II Series
025.428 S253

First Published 2021

Published by:
Ess Ess Publications
4831/24, Ansari Road, Darya Ganj, New Delhi-110 002, INDIA
Phones: 23260807, 41563444
Fax: 41563334
E-mail: info@essessreference.com
www.essessreference.com

Cover Design by *Patch Creative Unit*

Printed and bound in India

Charles Ammi Cutter

Dedicated with admiration and adoration to

Professor A. S. Chandel

A knowledgeable teacher, an experienced librarian

And the longest serving library professional in India

Contents

Preface

It is a popular misconception that book numbers have only a subsidiary role in library classification. That is why varied local,casual and substandard practices exist in libraries in their design and use. Most of the librarians take it to be an easy game of cursory sub-arrangement of documents by author's name within a specific broader class. Spawning local practices are rather demeaning, and standard practices are not observed fully or by the book. Advocates of book numbers genuinely feel that it gets step motherly treatment, both in theory and practice. As these are very essential for preparing library shelflists, many libraries either do not prepare shelflists, or prepare them in a faulty, lackadaisical manner. This ambivalent attitude only results in small pockets of chaos across the shelves.

The fact of the matter is that book numbers are indispensable for a fine, precise and overall logical arrangement of documents on the shelves. For shelf arrangement the function of book numbers begins from where that of the class numbers ends. To understand the importance of this functionality, an analogy would not be out of place. Just as in a long travel, the airplane, train, or the bus only get us near to our final destination then from where we have to take some local conveyance to reach home. In this analogy, the library classification is the plane (or other means of long distance public transportation) and the book number the local conveyance which would take the user direct and pin-pointedly to the document searched for. Incidentally the analogy of public and local also holds good as book numbers are mostly local.

Technically speaking, library classification is not only the marking of documents with relevant notation from any standard library classification system: it also means adding the correct book number for precise arrangement and granularly individualised location of documents in the library. Ranganathan always treated a book numbering system as a statutory part of library classification by formulating a Canon of Book Numbers[1]

The present book has a twofold task: First, it provides an authentic version of the Cutter-Sanborn three-figure table as in India many unauthorized versions of doubtful pedigree, even photocopied, are being used. For this purpose, its latest version, available in open access, has been downloaded from the Biblioteca UFRRJ/ITR website *https://academico.ufrrj.br/biblioteca/cutter/cutter6.html*. As is well known and often rued by many, all these tables are not suitable for Indian names. In fact, these were designed, and that not even scientifically, for American and European names. Problems faced by Indian and other Asian and African libraries in using these tables are common and genuine. To mitigate this problem a little, the table has been supplemented with Indian names. It may be made clear here that it is not any new table for Indian names, but only provides readymade cutter numbers for them as the librarians would have assigned them using the standard table. New names have been added at their alphabetical place for the librarians to readily use the table. It is a time saver. Personal and family names of all communities from all the regions have been taken from various library catalogues and books-in-prints. It also includes some corporate names and words likely to form a heading in library cataloguing. Some Western names have also been added in a row to facilitate Indian cataloguers.

But the more important purpose is to provide a manual for the use of cutter table and to prepare shelf lists, or to craft unique book numbers for various categories of documents and subjects, especially biographies, literary works, classics, and works of prolific authors. This remains the most neglected work in Indian libraries. This book addresses the problems of systematically creating unique book numbers and, consequently, the call numbers in such areas. This is by no means an easy task especially in the case of prolific writers, literary authors, classics and biographical publications. Book numbers not only have to sub-arrange, mostly alphabetically, the documents in a given specific class, but also to array them systematically. For example, autobiographies, diaries, memoirs of a person must file before the biographies of that luminary. Further, of necessity, the works by and on a person or on a single work must be filed side by side – host and the associated works must be brought together in a systematic way, especially in order of general to specifics within the same specific class number. This objective may require tweaking of rules or making adjustments, or taking some local decision and recording them in the authority file – the shelflist, in this case. Indian librarians are blissfully ignorant of such fine nuances in crafting book numbers.This book draws on such best practices as reported by John Comaromi[2] and Donald Lehnus[3] in their books which minutely and comprehensively take cases of systematically designing apt book numbers in the US libraries. Users of this book are suggested to consult these books for more in-depth studies and to tackle cases not taken up here. The singular aim is to amply illustrate the book numbering methods with examples of Indian subjects and authors.

Book numbering is a craft, a skill and a science which Indian librarians must learn and bring home to their library users the way knowledge is organized so nuancedly for them.

MPS

Notes

1. Ranganathan,S.R.(1967) "Canon of Book Number" In his: *Prolegomena to Library Classification*,3rd ed. Mumbai: Asia,Sec. UB2(p.503)
2. Comaromi, John. P. (1981) *Book Numbers: A Historical Study and Practical Guide to their Use.*Littleton, CO.: Libraries Unlimited, 145p.
3. Lehnus, D.J. (1980) *Book Numbers: History, Principles, and Application*, Chicago, Ill: American Library Association, iv, 153p.

Part I :
Origin and Development of Book Numbers

1

Life of Charles Ammi Cutter (1837-1903): The Prince of Librarianship

Until the early nineteenth century, librarianship was a profession,if at all it was, of a gentleman scholar, who presided over a library only with his vast learning. Love for books was the only qualification to be a library curator, as he was called then. Value of a library in a society and its role in educating the public and lifelong learning of an individual was being recognized in burgeoning democratic and industrial society of the United States of America. Education and books were proliferating. More libraries were needed for a growing literate population to keep them literate and aware citizens. Better professionally trained librarians were required to manage expanding library networks and their growing collections with an orientation to serve the patrons both with books and information. Big collections needed better organization. This milieu gave birth to the profession and political leaders who valued their libraries. Time was opportune for better and scientific management of libraries and their services. In 1876 the USA which celebrated her centenary as a nascent nation, was one such country. Charles Ammi Cutter was one such self-trained genius and a pioneer library leader. He formulated theories to standardise practice of librarianship only out of his experience, insights and vision. If Melvil Dewey (1851-1931) is the father of modern librarianship then Cutter with his varied and lasting contribution can safely be called the Prince of the Profession.

Charles Ammi was born on March 14, 1837 in Boston, Massachusetts in a merchant family. In his childhood he lived with his grandfather and two unmarried aunts who were cultured and devout Christians. They provided him access to best education of his time. Unitarian Church[1]was envisaged as the suited profession for this brilliant, but physically frail child with myopic eyes. Therefore, his early education was in classics and the Bible. In 1856 he entered the Harvard Divinity School from where he graduated after three years in 1859. He obtained best education of his times.While still at the Divinity School he was appointed student librarian from 1857-59.There he rearranged the collection and prepared its catalogue. This was an unintended entry into a profession wherein he rose like a star and became one of its immortal architect. Chief cataloguer Dr. Ezra Abbot (1819-1884)[2] being happy with his work got him appointed his assistant in the Harvard College library in 1860.There he worked diligently till the end of 1868. Ezra Abbot as his guide inspired Cutter for deep interest in cataloguing. Imbibed with the learning of his mentor and guide, Abbot, Cutter prepared a public catalogue on cards. It became the foundation of his later work at the Boston Athenaeum library (1869-1893) where he succeeded the famous William Fredrick Poole (1821-1894). Boston Athenaeum, founded in 1807 is one of the oldest and distinguished independent library in the USA. Today its collection of half a million volumes specializes in arts, literature, biography and history. It has made lasting contribution in the development of scholarship in the New England since early 19th century. Such a specialized library with high profile scholars as its users provided an apt laboratory and a fertile field for his work. At the Athenaeum he prepared a dictionary catalogue in a book form of the 100,000 strong collection of the library. The entire work which took eight years (1874-1882) was enshrined in five volumes running to 3042 pages. In order to prepare this catalogue according to standard and explicitly formulated rules he wrote his, now classic, *Rules for a Dictionary Catalogue* (1876) revised by him in 1889 and 1891. The fourth and last edition published posthumously was edited by his nephew William Parker Cutter, who was a librarian and later became his biographer. So enduring and influential is this work that very safely he can be described as the father of modern cataloguing. "All modern cataloguing rules are influenced by Cutter's rules…," writes a famous Professor John P.Immroth. The principles he formulated for vocabulary control are still applied in subject cataloguing tools like the *Library of Congress Subject Headings* and the *Sears List of Subject Headings* and taught in library schools across the world.

In 1893 Cutter resigned from the Boston Athenaeum to become librarian of the newly established Forbes Library, Northampton, MA in 1894. There he experimented with his theories of library administration and services. New services were initiated of lending books, non-book material and realia to a wider community of users, and developed innovative exchange and extension programmes with other libraries.

Today, Cutter is remembered mostly for his three major contributions: the other two being the *Expansive Classification* (EC) and the Cutter author tables. The EC (1891-1903) was developed due to his disliking for Dewey's decimal system (1876). Instead of a pure notation of the decimal numbers, he employed alphabets to denote main classes and numerals for further divisions. Since then many a classification systems have used this kind of alpha-numeric mixed notation, which is more suitable for an ever growing universe of knowledge. The scheme consisted of seven schedules, or expansions, each contained in a separate volume, and had more details over the previous one. The first expansion was meant for, say a village library with a small collection, the seventh for a university or a national library. However, Cutter died before completing the seventh volume. In some ways it was considered more logical and scientific than the Dewey's system, though it could not replace it. This classification had many innovative and commendable features which were incorporated by the Library of Congress Classification (1903+). H. E. Bliss (1870-1955) also adopted some of its features in his *Bibliographic Classification* (1940-53). No wonder then it has been described as classifier's classification, and a stepping-stone to future classification systems.

In connection with the *Expansive Classification,* Cutter devised a system of abbreviations for the names of authors or headings to be used for sub arranging books on the shelves having the same class number, call it book numbering. Developed in the form of author table, it was a simple alphanumeric code standing for the heading under which the publication is catalogued, usually, a name be it of a person, corporate body, geographic entity or title of the book. Today, many versions of Cutter tables are available, and the terms cutter or cuttering have become eponyms for alphabetical book numbering methods.

Cataloguing and classification were not his only contributions to the then emerging discipline of library science. With other professional giants like Melvil Dewey, he founded and nurtured the American Library Association in 1876, and remained its President from 1887 to 1889. The ALA rose to become the largest and most powerful library association in the world. Also with Dewey he founded the *Library Journal* and edited it from 1881-1893 and gave it a new lease of life with his scholarly and aptly topical editorials. Finally he contributed towards the development and maturation of the then burgeoning library education by providing a body of defined knowledge and science to impart it. He is a founding father of library science.

He died on September 6, 1903 leaving behind his wife Sarah whom he had married in 1863, and two engineer sons, Louis and Roland. A person of cheerful disposition he was frank, honest with a strong capacity for friendship, writes his nephew William Parker Cutter. He played hard, was fond of walking, cycling, driving, boating, theatre, music and concerts. He loved good food and good wine. Alive to everything fine and good, he enjoyed and loved life and nature —the sun, stars, rain and the mountains. This simple and sweet tempered man with a strong sense of humour was considerate, modest and a savant, a typical New Englander.

Notes

1. Unitarianism is a Christian belief that God is a single entity and not three forms as expressed in the Trinity. Unitarian Churches follow the doctrine of Unitarianism and are organized in the United States and the United Kingdom on a national and local level. www.christianity.com/church/denominations/what...
2. Ezra Abbot, born at Cambridge, Massachusetts, was an American Biblical scholar. As assistant librarian of Harvard University from 1856 to 1872 he planned and perfected an alphabetical card catalogue, combining many of the advantages of the ordinary dictionary catalogues with the grouping of the minor topics under more general heads, which is characteristic of a systematic catalogue. From 1872 until his death he was Bussey Professor of New Testament Criticism and Interpretation in the Harvard Divinity School. He was one of the 32 founding members of the Society of Biblical Literature in 1880

References

Cutter, William Parker.*Charles Ammi Cutter*. Chicago: ALA, 1931, 67p. (Later reissued by Gress Press, Boston,1972)

Immroth, John Phillip "Cutter, Charles Ammi (1837-1903)" In *Encyclopedia of library and information science/* ed. by Allen Kent, *et al.* New York: Marcel Dekker, 1971, pp. 380-387.

Maltby, Arthur. *Sayers manual of classification for librarians*, 5th ed. London: Andre Deutsch, 1975, pp. 123-125.

Miksa, Francis L. "Cutter, Charles Ammi (1837-1903)" In *ALA world encyclopedia of library and information services* ed. by R. Wedgeworth, 2nd ed. Chicago: ALA, 1986, pp.238-240.

Satija, M.P. "Book number and call number" In *Encyclopedia of library and information science/* ed. by Allen Kent, *et al*. New York: Marcel Dekker, Vol.45, 1990, pp.18-45.

www.bostonatheneum.org/general /html (Accessed on 15th April 2020).

2

Cutter–Sanborn Table : A Brief History

Origin and development of book numbers is coeval with the relative classification begun by Melvil Dewey (1851-1931) in 1873 with what is now known by the Dewey Decimal Classification. Now all the library classifications, which have come up in its wake and are relative in nature, require book numbers to sub arrange documents having the same class number. At the Amherst College, Melvil Dewey, who was the first to confront the problem of sub arrangement, did so by numbering books 1,2,3…so on within the same class in the order these were accessioned in the library. This sub arrangement broadly resulted in the chronological order of their acquisition in the library irrespective of the year of publication. Another proposal was to sub arrange alphabetically by the name of the author. Soon someone suggested to convert names into numbers for convenience of handling. A prototype, actually a part of his 'combined system' of classification was devised in 1878 by M. Jacob Schwartz(1846-1926), then librarian of New York Apprentices' Library of Philadelphia from 1871-1900. His system sub arranged books first by size and then by author. C A. Cutter extolled Schwartz's book numbers over Dewey's accession method, as he thought that the accession arrangement yielded neither logical sub-arrangement nor was of any mnemonic aid in retrieval. Cutter, by way of further simplification, proposed a book numbering system which totally disregarded the book size, and suggested that the numerals be decimal numbers for future insertion of new names and numbers. Thus there was a simple and mnemonic method to convert author names into decimal numbers. His original scheme is given below

A-Bo	0	M	5
Br-C	1	N-R	6
D-F	2	S	7
G-H	3	T-V	8
I-L	4	W-Z	9

Thus any name, say, with E will get the author number 2, and with S would receive the number 7. As decimal numbers, these could be expanded to distinguish two or more authors whose surname started with the same initial letter. For example, Gray could be given 32, and for Gordon it could be expanded to 320

Late in the nineteenth century, many new and ingenious book numbering ideas flooded the classification horizon. It was then a current, very relevant and favourite topic of study and deliberation. In its February 1879 issue, the incipient *Library Journal* published a symposium ("Plans for Numbering, with Special Reference to Fiction: A Library Symposium," *Libr. Jl.*, 4, 38-47) on book numbers by leading librarians such as Melvil Dewey, C. A. Cutter, Josephus Nelson Larned (Librarian, Young Men's Association Library, Buffalo), John Edmands (Librarian, Philadelphia Mercantile Library), and John Fitzpatrick (Librarian, Bronson Library, Waterbury, Connecticut). Here John Edmands (1820-1915) made an everlasting contribution to book numbers by suggesting that the author's initial letter be followed by decimal notation for rest of the letters in the name which would represent the complete name. The number could thus at least suggest vaguely the author's name. Cutter at first objected to Edmands' idea, fearing perhaps that it would again promiscuously mix the class number and the book number. He rather preferred alphabets for class numbers and pure decimal numbers for book numbers. However, Cutter relented, realizing the merits of Edmands' suggestion. C. A. Cutter was later to take Edmands' method to a highly developed system by which Cutter is today eminently known, and which has earned him a place in the annals of English language and world librarianship. Here Cutter made three enduring contributions:

1. In transcription, book numbers were distinguished from class numbers.
2. By rejecting book size as a characteristic of sub-arrangement, Cutter emancipated classification from the size shackles inherited from the relatively dark ages in classification
3. More importantly, he introduced decimal notation for author numbers to intercalate new names and to expand the existing ones

Cutter was also the first to fully design, publish and sell an author table in 1880 from Boston. By 1882 Dewey was already using Cutter's author table.

At the annual conference of the American Library Association held on September 25, 1885, Dewey reaffirmed the mnemonic value of mixed notation of letters and numerals as "the best plan I can conceive for alphabetical arrangement, and I hope someone will make the necessary table for applying it". This "someone" was to be Charles Ammi Cutter. Very soon after the 1879 symposium, Cutter in 1880 devised a table for author numbers for commercial sale as advertised in the *Library Journal* (September-October 5, 1880; 293). This table, the first of a long line of Cutter tables, was based on his experience of classification at the Boston Athenaeum. Of this table, now non-extant, John Comaromi surmises: that "was probably composed... of three pieces of paste board held together by cloth tape". Its 1888 version is available whose extract is reproduced below:

Ger	31	Have	Ac	1	Ar	Sa	1	Sh
Gerr	32	Hax	Aid	2	Arc	Sai	2	Sha
Gess	33	Hayf	Aig	3	Are	Sal	3	She

As per instructions any name/word beginning with a consonant (except S) requires one initial letter followed by two numbers from the table. For example,

Beard	B 34	Holmes	H 73
Browning	B 82	Huxley	H98
Churchill	C 47	Lewis	L 58
Franklin	F 85	Russell	R 91
Grahm	G 76	Tennyson	T 25
Hay	H 32		

A word beginning with a vowel or S requires first two letters followed by a single digit:

Abbot	Ab 2	Olney	Ol 6
Anne	An 7	Upton	Up 1
Edwards	Ed 9	Sinclair	Si 6
Ives	Iv 3	Smith	Sm5

Similarly, the author number for any word beginning with Sc consists of three initial letters followed by one digit. And li, lw, lx, ly, Oo, Uo, Uq, Uu, Ss, and Sx are used without any numerical digit following them, obviously as English names beginning with the above letters, except Li and Ly, are rare. Several versions of this table are available printed up to 1886. Originally known as Cutter's Alfabetic-Order Table, it is now known as Cutter's Two-Figure Author Table. Instructions for using the table were made available in a separate booklet, which was also published in different sources. By the mid-1880s, Cutter tables had become quite popular, and many librarians including Melvil Dewey swore by their usefulness at various fora. Approval of as commanding a personality as Dewey imparted to it an added momentum. A noteworthy feature of the table was that the distribution of numbers to names was based somewhat on their statistical frequency of occurrence, though the process was not carried to perfection.

Cutter-Sanborn Table

Cutter's two-figure table suitable for small libraries was found inadequate for large classes of fiction and individual biography. To meet the need of large and rapidly expanding libraries (there were many), Cutter decided to expand his table to three figures and add more names. In 1892, the revision was entrusted to Miss Kate Emery Sanborn (1860-1951) (later married to M. Gardner Jones (1850-1941) who was librarian of Salem, Massachusetts Public Library). Kate was Cutter's assistant and a cataloguer at Boston Athenaeum from 1883 to 1891. Miss Sanborn was then working as a cataloguer from 1891-1894 at the Mercantile Library, St. Louis so could not work under Cutter's direct supervision. (Kate ultimately served from 1894-1897 as librarian of the Manchester (New Hampshire) Public Library). Being away from Cutter the result was virtually an independent, albeit greatly improved, work by all accounts and assessment. The revised work was published in two parts initially. The first part for six letters only, namely vowels A, E, I, O, U and S, was published and sold by C. A. Cutter in 1892. The table for the remaining 20 consonants was made available in 1895. Later these two were consolidated into a single table. This complete table contains more than 12,000 author numbers, 12361 entries to be exact.

This is known as the Cutter-Sanborn Three-Figure Author Table, wherein a few numbers betray ancestry to Cutter's Two-Figure Author Table. In this table, regardless of any initial letter including vowels and S, every author number uniformly begins with one letter followed by a decimal digit varying from one to three: two digits for the letters E, I, O, J, K, Y, and Z; one digit for letters Q and X; all other letters use three decimal digits. Uniformity in the use of only one initial letter for every name came as a great relief to cataloguers. In addition, it is a scientifically constructed table with better correlation between the quantity of numbers assigned to each letter of the alphabet and the frequency of names beginning with each letter. For all its virtues, this table met with almost instant success, and its popularity continues unabated today. Of all the versions of Cutter tables, two-thirds sold are those of Cutter-Sanborn affiliation.

Cutter had asked Miss Sanborn only to expand the table to three figures, whereas she produced an independent work which could not be used by the libraries using Cutter's two-figure table to expand the existing author numbers. Thus his two-figure table was falling into disuse. This so disturbed and irked Cutter that he tried to repudiate the new work; and set to revising the two-figure author table himself. (From 1895 to 1901 the only three-figure table that was available was the Cutter-Sanborn). Cutter devised a three-figure author table of solely his own which was ready for sale by January 1902. It has more than 20,800 names and numbers. Cutter did much to promote the sale of his new table --but to little avail. By that time the Cutter-Sanborn table had become well entrenched. A survey of book numbers in the USA in 1996 found that about 52% of the book numbers were based on Cutter-Sanborn, whereas 37% still used Cutter Table. It is an irony of life that a work which Cutter once described as a mistake and even tried to disown, is the major living and applied work associated with his name today.

Cutter's new table was not well planned and consequently inconsistent: A, E, Q, S, X, Y, Z used two digits; I, O, U were followed by one digit; and for all other letters the number of digits varied from one to three; the letter X with two different sets of numbers confused many. Moreover the mechanics of the distribution of the numbers over the names is not explained. In fact it is not based on any statistical method of distributing names to numbers. He did not make any use of telephone directories for this purpose. The much disliked convention of using the first two letters for the words beginning with vowels or S and three letters for names beginning with Sc still persisted:

Atchison	At 24	Maugham	M 442
Clark	C 547	Pope	P 811
Dewey	D 525	Simpson	Si 58
Dickinso	D 555	Smith	Sm 52
Dragon	D 787	Schwartz	Sch 82
Edward	Ed 98	Thackeray	T 325
Hughes	H 874	Washington	W 277
Mann, T	M 315	Zaidenberg	Z 13

However, this table is still in use as evidenced by the reprinting of the major three versions of his tables in 1969, reset with modifications and reprinted in unbroken A/Z order of two columns with letters on the left with their corresponding numbers against them on the right. These were edited by Esther M. Swift and Paul K. Swanson. It is highly significant that Paul K. Swanson is from the Forbes Library, Northampton, Massachusetts, where Cutter served as founder librarian from 1894 to 1903. Esther M. Swift is the Editor of H. R. Huntting Company, Inc., Chicopee, Massachusetts, distributor of the tables from 1964 to 1979. Today these tables are distributed by Libraries Unlimited of Littleton, Colorado. Another version of the Swnson-Swift revision of Cutter-Sanborn three figure author table is published by Hargrove House, Littleton, CO, USA (www.cuttertables.com). Richard Ammi Cutter, grandson of C. A. Cutter, holds the present copyright. Mounted on board and bound with sturdy covers in metal spiral binding, physically and typographically these are much improved editions. Swanson-Swift revisions have better publication standards with some minor corrections. The rearrangement in a single unbroken sequence of alphabets makes the tables easier to use. Inevitably, these editions are welcome in libraries using in-house typed and worn out copies for want of any commercially distributed versions commensurate with the high demand, though the Cutter-Sanborn table was also reprinted and distributed in 1969 by H. R. Hunting Inc. In the absence of the availability of any authentic edition, many spuriously reproduced editions have been marketed. Swanson-Swift versions may stem this tide of unauthorized versions. Now Cutter-Sanborn table is also available on the Web as open source at *http://ub.uibk.ac.at/fbg/author/author5.htm*. Some excerpts from these tables taken from some alphabets are reproduced below:

A	S	O	Z
111 Aa	111 Sa	11 Oa	11 Za
112 Aal	112 Saar	12 Ob	12 Zab
113 Aar	113 Sab	13 Obr	13 Zac
114 Aars	114 Sabb	14 Obs	14 Zacco
115 Aas	115 Sabe	15 Oc	15 Zach
116 Aba	116 Sabi	16 Och	16 Zachar
117 Abal	117 Sabl	17 Oco	17 Zacu
118 Abar	118 Sabr	18 Oconn	18 Zag
119 Abat	119 Sac	19 Ocor	19 Zah
121 Abau	121 Sach	21 Oct	21 Zai
122 Abb	122 Saco	22 Od	22 Zal
123 Abbat	123 Sacr	23 Ode	23 Zam
124 Abbe	124 Sad	24 Odi	24 Zambo
125 Abbo	125 Sade	25 Odo	25 Zamo
126 Abbot	126 Sadl	26 Odon	26 Zamp
127 Abbot, J.	127 Sae	27 Odr	27 Zan
128 Abbot, M	128 Saf	28 Oe	28 Zane
129 Abbot, S.	129 Sag	29 Oer	29 Zang

Cutter-Sanborn has become a standard and will continue to be so in the foreseeable future

Current Trends

The book numbers had had their golden period from the late 19th to the first decade of the 20th century. After that only innovative work was of S. R. Ranganathan who proposed a very ingenious and comprehensive chronological system for all editions of Colon Classification in 1933/1987. By then the shelf-listing procedures had become a passé art. Of course it was practiced but did not make any innovation. Published literature was only descriptive of prevailing practices. Again in 1980s there was a small spurt of interest with the publication of two important textbooks by Donald J. Lehnus (1980) and John P. Comaromi (1981) covering almost the same ground of the US practices in shelflisting. The age of electronic information almost assumed the end of road for them. But such gloomy predictions have not proved true. No doubt, bar-coding/RFID may serve some of the purpose of book numbers to distinguish one store-item from the other — howsoever similar. But in hybrid libraries with growing collections of prints and other information bearing objects (IBOs) some device for discrete and granular sub arrangement of the items will always be needed. There the book numbers are still indispensable. It has been rightly pointed out in the OCLC report (O'Neill, *et al,* 1996) that "The resolution power of the cutter tables has diminished due to growth in library collections and the increasing incidence of corporate names and title main entries". It has always been seen that it often requires adjustment and manual processing to prevent shelf list conflicts and cluttering on the shelves to provide a unique call numbers to each document. To meet such situations the OCLC has expanded the cutter tables to "balance the distributions of main entries over the cutter table entries." Electronic version available at *www.oclc.org/dewey* is compatible with existing two figure or three figure tables. It provides readymade cutter numbers by just filling in the name/heading for which the cutter mark is required. This table is versatile and also facilities algorithmic cuttering. It is clear that book numbers are expecting a revival of interest though on a small scale in the new information environment. Watch out the emerging trend in designing expert systems for cutter numbers (Savic,1996).

Appendix

Original Cutter Tables

1. C.A. Cutter's Alphabetic Order Table. Alternatives for the Vowels and S. Altered and Fitted with Three Figures, by Kate E. Sanborn, Library Bureau, Boston, 1892.4pp.of Tables, 33x17 cm.
2. C.A. Cutter's alphabetic Order Tables-Consonants Except S. Altered and Fitted with Three-Figures, by Kate E. Sanborn, Library Bureau, Boston, 1895, 14pp. of Tables, 33x28 cm.
3. C.A. Cutter's alphabetic Order Table Consonants Except S. and Vowels and S. Altered and Fitted with Three-Figures, by Kate E. Sanborn, Library Bureau, Boston, 1896, 18pp. of Tables, 13x15 cm.

Various Cutter tables in print now

4. C. A. Cutter's Two Figure Author Table, Swanson-Swift Revision 1969, H.R. Huntting Co., Chicopee, MA, 1969, 29 pp, 39x29 cm.
5. C. A. Cutter's Three Figure Author Table, Swanson-Swift Revision 1969, H.R. Huntting Co., Chicopee, MA, 1969, 29 pp, 39x29 cm.
6. Cutter-Sanborn Three Figure Author Table, Swanson-Swift Revision 1969, H.R. Huntting Co., Chicopee, MA, 1969, 33 pp, 39x22 cm.
7. Cutter-Sanborn Three Figure Author Table, Huntting Co., Chicopee, MA (Distributors), 1964, 8 pp, 35 cm.

Sources: Some historical articles on book numbers

M. Dewey, "Plans for Numbering, with Special Reference to Fiction: A Library Symposium," *Libr. J.*, 4, 38-47 (February 1879), p.47.

A.P. Massey, "Classification of Fiction," *Libr. J.*, 6, 7-9 (January 1881).

C. A. Cutter, Boston Athenaeum: How to Get Books with an Explanation of the New Way of Marking Books. Press of Rockwell and Churchill, Boston, 1882, pp. 14-15.

"Dui's Doings," *Libr. J.*, 7, 237 (September 1882).

M. Dewey. "Remarks in the Proceedings of the ALA Buffalo Conference, August 14, 1883," *Libr. Jl.*, 8, 275 (September/ October 1883).

C. A. Cutter, "How to Use Cutter's Decimal Author Tables," *Libr. J.*, 12, 251-252 (July 1887); 549 (December 1887).

C. R. Olin, "An Order Table for Collective Biography," *Libr. J.*, 18, 144 (May 1893).

H.E. Bliss, "Simplified Book Notation," *Libr. J.*, 35, 545 (1910).

H.E. Bliss, "A Simplified Alphabetic Order Table," *Libr. J.*, 37, 71-72 (1912).

Z. Brown, "More About Cutter Numbers," *Libr.J.*, 57, 437 (1932).

First two full books on book numbers

1. A.C. Laws, *Author Notation in the Library of Congress*, Government Printing Office, Washington, D.C., 1917, p. 18.
2. B.R. Barden, *Book Numbers: A Manual for Students with a Basic Code of Rules*, American Library Association, Chicago, 1937, p.7.

Modern books on book numbers

D. J. Lehnus : *Book Numbers : History, Principles, and Application*, American Library Association, Chicago, 1980. iv, 153p.

J. P. Comaromi : *Book Numbers : A Historical Study and Practical Guide to their Use*, Libraries Unlimited, Littleton, CO, 1981, 145p.

M. P. Satija and J. P. Comaromi: *Beyond Classification: Book Numbers with Special Reference to Chronological Book Numbers*. Ess Ess Publicartions, New Delhi 1992, xi,115p

M. P. Satija : *Book numbers: Indian and Cutter*. Viva Books, New Delhi, 2008, xi, 132p.

Some current articles on book numbers

William Denton, "Book Numbers" Feb 2003. *htttp://www.miskatonic.org/library/book- numbers.html(Accessed on 15 May, 2020)*

Edward T. O'Neill, *et al*, "Four-Figure Cutter Tables" (1996) , p. 4. *http://digitalarchive.oclc.org/da/ ViewObjectMain.jsp?objid= 0000003355&frame=true. (Accessed on 15 May 2020).*

M. P. Satija, "History of Book Numbers," *Int. Classif.*, 14(2), Sec 6 (1987). This paper also explains some Indian cuttering procedures; and catalogues some unauthorized editions of Cutter-Sanborn tables published in India.

Dobrica Savic, "Cutt-x: An Expert System for Automatic Assignment of Cutter Numbers", *Cat &Classif Qly* 22(2), 71-87(1996).

Part II :
Using the Table and Preparing Shelflist

3

How to Use Cutter-Sanborn Table for Shelflisting

Introduction

Book numbers are a satellite of class numbers as these are only required in relative classification first devised by Melvil Dewey. Pre-Dewey fixed location systems did not require them. A book number is a devise for sub arrangement of documents on library shelves having the same class number. Thus it is classification within classification —a classificatory step beyond subject groupings. To give another analogy: take the location of the book in a library as the destination to be arrived at. Here the class number represents the highway travel, and the book number the local conveyance. A book number is an integral constituent of a call number which determines the unique place of the document on the shelves. The call number for a document is unique to it in a given library

Call Number = Collection Number+Class Number+Book Number

Sub-arrangement with book numbers may be alphabetical mostly by the heading under which the book has been catalogued or it could be chronological by the year of publication —latter method is preferred by S. R. Ranganthan who devised a very sophisticated book numbering system for his Colon Classification (Satija, 2008, 55-90). This chapter only dwells on the book numbering procedure with the Cutter-Sanborn three figure table –latter, as given in chapter 4, has been supplemented with Indian names for the convenience and ready reference in Indian libraries. It is to illustrate and amply exemplify the process of shelf-listing and book numbering in many grey areas for consistently logical arrangements of documents, and to bring the host and its associated books together on the shelves using the Dewey's classification and the Cutter-Sanborn table.

Facile Simplicity

Contrary to popular perceptions, or the erroneous practices in Indian libraries, book numbering is not an easy or facile process of marking and parking from any of the Cutter tables. It is much more than that: a process which requires fine-tuned manual precision in assigning a book number. **It is quite possible that a same author may get slightly different book numbers in different classes in the same library**. Book numbers have to be very carefully assigned every time consulting the library's shelf list. In this way book numbering and shelf listing procedures have hand in glove relationship.

In case of literary authors, prolific authors, biographies, genealogies, bibliographies and classics to keep the host and associated books together many a devices have to be employed, and a lot of local adjustments have to be made. It makes book numbering a challenging and interesting work.

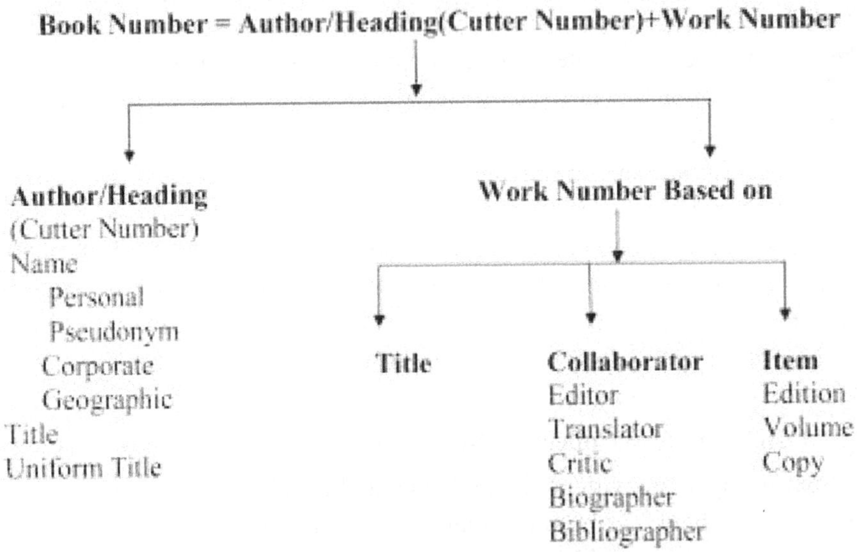

Functions of Book Numbers

Function of a book number starts from where that of the class number ends. Book numbers individualize a book so that it " may be quickly and accurately placed, called for, found and charged" wrote Melvil Dewey (1885) in the second edition of his classification system. Miss Bertha R. Barden(1937) in her enduring study of book numbers has described the following six uses of book numbers which are wonderfully valid to this day:

1. To arrange books in order on the shelves.
2. To provide a brief and unique call number for each book.
3. To precisely locate a particular book on the shelf.
4. Provide a symbol for charging books to borrowers.
5. To facilitate the return of books on the shelves.
6. To assist in quick identification of a book when inventories are taken. It helps in stock-taking.

We can add three more important uses of book numbers, viz.,

7. Book numbers are indispensable for shelf-listing.
8. An author number also brings together all the books by one author in one specific subject.
9. In case of literary books, classics and biographical works the book numbers bring together commentaries, critical studies and translations and other associated works with the host book.

A chronological book number will clearly portray the development of a subject over a given period

The four basic purposes of book numbers as given by Donald J. Lehnus (1980, 75-76) are to:

"1. Sub arranges the materials with the same classification number in a systematic and logical order.

"2. Assign to each item a distinctive group of symbols, that is, a call number that will distinguish it from all others in the collection.

"3. Provide a call number that facilitates finding a particular item among all the others in the collection and returning it to the same relative location.

"4. Maintain an accurate record of loaned items, or items that are temporarily away from their normal position, such as books placed in a reserve reading collection or that have been sent to the bindery".

Shelflist

A shelf-list (also called shelf catalogue) is a record of catalogued items in a library arranged in the shelf order of documents –that is classified. Though mostly for internal use of the staff, a shelf-list has varied purposes from inventory control to collection editing. To make a call number unique, precise book numbers are crafted for preparing shelflists —it is a dynamic and evolving tool (Carter, 1970, 334). In fact book numbering and shelf listing are locked in a relation of mutual dependence, as said earlier. Shelf-lists cannot be prepared without book numbers, and for assigning precise book numbers the shelf list has to be invariably consulted every time. John Comaromi (1981, 29) aptly warns that value of the shelflist should not be undermined.

Shelf-list *vs* Library Catalogue

- A catalogue is a public document for the use of the library patrons.
- A shelf-list is ordinarily prepared as a working tool for the internal use of the staff in the technical section.
- A shelf-list has one entry for each bibliographic item whereas the catalogue has multiple access points.
- However a shelf-list enshrines much more information than in the OPAC entry, that is it may include accession number, date and source of acquisition, price of the item, location and condition of individual copies and some notes as missing, etc.
- Copy numbers may not be given on the OPAC entries, but these are invariably mentioned in the shelf-list entries, e.g., for two copies of the *Prolegomena to library classification* by S R Ranganathan

  025.43 R196P c.1 025.43 R196P c.2
- In case the library is using a dictionary catalogue then a shelf list may also provide the classified approach for subject access in libraries. In the absence of a classified catalogue the shelflist "spreads before the scholar's eyes what a library possesses in their fields of study" Comaromi (1981, 29).
- It may be used in preparing subject bibliographies by the class number.
- In this way the dictionary catalogue is looked upon as index of the shelf-list.
- According to Ruth Carter (1970, 333) a library's shelflist can serve as a "guide to material selection, because it facilitates the determination of the extent of collection in any specified subject area. Measurements of shelflists can be a method of comparative evaluation of the collections of similar libraries, particularly research libraries"
- A machine readable shelf list may be used as a database for generating many byproducts such as current aware lists, and classified bibliographies on demand.

How to Use the Cutter-Sanborn Table

There is not much difference in how to use the various versions of Cutter tables.

Here the use of the Cutter-Sanborn table is described briefly. To assign a Cutter number, determine the first word of the heading (it could be a place name, personal or corporate name, or the title) and locate the number corresponding to it in the table under that alphabet. When a number has been found, it is to be preceded by the initial letter of the heading. This will be the Cutter number —first and primary part of the book number. For example, John Abbott will have the Cutter number A 127. **But more often than not there will be no number to fit the name heading congruously**. In that case, the closest approximation to that number will be taken, for example, Maxwell will be M 465, and Macbeth M 118. Usually a heading will fall between two words in the table, in such a case the lower number of the two is to be assigned. For example, a name Peh, which has not been enumerated, falls between Peg 376 and Pei 377, will be denoted by P376. Similarly a cutter number for any word or combination of letters may be assigned:

Chaucer	C 496	India	I 39	Cambridge	C 178
Hardy, T	H 272	Panama	P 187	International	I 41

Crafting Book Numbers

As said earlier, cutter number is the primary and first part of a book number. In many cases we have to add item number to it for completing a book number.

Book number = Author/heading number (cutter number) + Item number.

Item number (also called work number) is that part of the book number which denotes a specific individual item having the same cutter number. Item number at times is problematic in assigning like a tail wagging the dog. **Nevertheless, not all documents need to have the item number,** e.g.,

Library Administration by S. R. Ranganathan 025.1 R196. Here no item number is required as Ranganathan wrote no other book having the class number 025.1. But item number is required for following books on classification by S. R. Ranganathan:

Classification and Communication 024.43 R196C (C is the item number)

Elements of Classification 025.43 R196E

Elements of Classification/revised by B I Palmer 025.43 R196EP (Here EP is the item number and P stands for Palmer, and thus both the editions of the *Elements* will file together).

Prolegomena to Library Classification 025.43 R196P

Prolegomena to Library Classification, 3rd ed.(1967) 025.43 R196P3 (here 3 is for the 3rd edition)

But *Philosophy of Classification* 025.43001 R196 (Here no item number is required as Ranganathan wrote only one book having the class number 025.43001).

D.J. Lehnus (1980,76-77) provides three rudiments which must be followed in the formation of book numbers and designing shelflists:

"1. It is necessary to consult the shelf list before assigning a book number in order to avoid the problem of having different publications with identical call numbers. Also, by consulting the shelf list it is easier to assign the simplest, but yet the most appropriate book number in relation to all other materials already classified with the same classification number.

"2. The length and detail of each book number depends on the number of items with the same classification number. Thus, if there are many items with the same classification number, the book number will necessarily have to be longer and more detailed.

"3. Book numbers are always considered as decimals. In this way, new numbers can be intercalated indefinitely and an alphabetical order is always maintained."

Popular Names

If there are two or more authors with the same surname having the same class number, then these may be differentiated by decimally extending a number by a digit for one author —it may be remembered that cutter numbers are decimal fractions and can be extended. **"Every author should be assigned only one book number under each classification number, but the same author will not have the same book number assigned to other works."** (Lehnus,1980,79). This is a manual adjustment varying from library to library, e.g., Aldous Huxley H986 and Thomas Huxley H 9865, if a library has books by both in the same specific class.

Let us suppose there are two names Ranganathan and Rangaswamy who have written books having the same class number then we may extend the three figure decimal number for Rangaswamy who also wrote on cataloguing like Ranganathan:

Ranganathan: Cataloguing 025.42 R196

Rangaswamy: Cataloguing 025.42 R1965.

But if a book on cataloguing by a new author Rangarajan is acquired in the library then it may be given the extended cutter number 025.42 R1963. All the three books will file alphabetically. Later let us suppose another book on cataloguing authored by V.K Rangachari is acquired in the library. To file it before Ranganathan, we will assign it the number R1955. Thus the ultimate order will be

Rangachari: Cataloguing	025.42 R1955
Ranganathan: Cataloguing	025.42 R196

Rangangarajan: Cataloguing 025.42 R1963

Rangaswamy: Cataloguing 025.42 R1965

But, say, V.K. Rangachari writing in the class 025.2, where there is no such closeness of names, will be given the usual author number R196. Indeed many local adjustments have to be made in case of popular names such as Iyer, Sharma, Singh, Kapoor, Kumar, Pandey, Mishra, Yadav, Prasad, Mukherjee, Patel, Ranga…,Swaminathan, Subra.... The difficulty is compounded as the Cutter tables were not designed for non-European names.

Author Numbers for Biographical Works

As said earlier, assigning book numbers is not a facile or mechanical work, especially for biographical works. Such works in a library may be categories as follow:

1. Collective biographies such as biographical dictionaries, or any collection of more than three biographies
2. Family histories or genealogies.
3. Autobiographies, reminiscences, memoirs, diaries
4. Biographies,

Collective biographies are to be treated as ordinary books : *Ten great economists: From Marx to Keynes* by Joseph A. Schumpeter 330.092 S392.

- In the case of individual biographies, genealogies, family histories, it is not the author but the biographee (subject) which is used for cutter number designation.
- For, biographies and family histories the work number (item number) is derived from the name of the writer (not from the title).

In this way all biographies of one person are arranged alphabetically by the name of the biographer, i.e. author.

A Unique Case

Let's take a very unique case of biographies of a famous family whose members have autobiography, individual biographies, and a book on family history:

The Kapoors: The First Family of Indian Cinema by Madhu Jain (2005) 791.43092 K17

KhullamKhulla: Rishi Kapoor Uncensored (2017) (with Meena Iyer): An autobiography 791.43092 K17

Raj Kapoor by Ritu Nanda (2017) 791.43092 K17

Shashi Kapoor, the Householder, the Star by Aseem Chhabra (2016) 791.43092 K17.

How to arrange them together in a logical way? Of course, the family history comes first. For the rest there are many options. Let us arrange them alphabetically by name of the subject (biographee). Then the alphabetical order will be Raj, Rishi and Shashi. These individual names can be used as second cutter number

Raj Kapoor 791.43092 K17 R161

Rishi Kapoor 791.43092 K17 R595

Shashi Kapoor 791.43092 K17 S612

We can even shorten the second cutter numbers to R1, R5, and S6 respectively. All these number will be preceded by the number 791.43092 K17 which is for the Kapoor's family history in general. The problem does not end here. There may be another biography of Raj Kapoor by Craig Harris. Then it will also require another item number for Harris. Its call number may be Raj Kapoor 791.43092 K17 R161 H313, and it will file after Ritu Nanda's work.

More Examples

For example, the biography of Winston Churchill (by Robert Balch) will have the cutter number C563. Similarly, the Life of Benjamin Franklin by V. Adams will be given number F831. This will help to bring together at one place all the biographies of a luminary. The various biographies of a person may be further distinguished by author's name, e.g.:

Life of W. Churchill by R. Balch	B	C563B
Biography of Churchill by Mark Smith	B	C563S
Life of Benjamin Franklin by V. Adams	B	F831A
Benjamin Franklin by B. D. Maurice.	B	F831M

(Here B is the class number for biography)

Ramanujan :The Man and the Mathematician by S R Ranganathan 510.924 R165R (here R165 is for Ramanujan, and the latter R is for Ranganathan to distinguish various biographies of Srinivas Ramanujan). Similarly,

Gurudev Rabindranath Tagore: A Biography by R.Sigi B T128S

Prermchand: A Life by Amrit Rai B P925A

If further needed, (e.g., if a person has written two different biographies of the same person) the work number i.e. initial letter of the title may be added, e.g.,

Life of Churchill by Balch C563BL (L stands for Life)

Winston Churchill by Balch C563BW (W stands for Winston)

Let us take a few more examples:

S. R. Ranganathan : an intellectual biography/ by Girja Kumar 020.924 R196G

S. R. Ranganathan : a short biography/ by Indian Statistical Institute 020.924 R196I

S. R. Ranganathan,1892-1972, edited by Edward Dudley 020.924 R196S (here S is from the S R, the heading under which the book should be catalogued according to the AACR2)

S. R. Ranganathan: *pragmatic philosopher of information science/* by T. R. Yogeshwar 020.924 R196Y

So all the biographical works on Ranganathan will come together on the shelves. But autobiographies are not given any work number, e.g., *A librarian looks back* (autobiography of S R Ranganathan) 020.924 R196. In this way the autobiography will file before all his biographies.

Prolific Authors

Work number may also be required if a person has written two or more books having the same class number, e.g.,

Prolegomena to library classification by S R Ranganathan 025.43 R196P

Prolegomena to library classification, 3rd ed.(1967) by S R Ranganathan 025.43 R196P3 (here P3 means the 3rd edition of the *Prolegomena*)

Classification and communication by S R Ranganathan 025.43 R196C

Elements of library classification by S R Ranganathan 025.43 R196E

Ranganathan's *Elements of library classification*, edited by B I Palmer 025.43 R196EP*.

*(In this case P denotes Palmer, thus both the editions of the *Elements* will come together on the shelf).

Bibliographies

Personal bibliographies are arranged not by the compiler but by the person whose works (both by and on) are bibliographed:

A bibliography on Mahatma Gandhi /by Dr. J. S.Sharma 012 G195 S (Here S is for Sharma, the compiler)

An Essay in Personal Bibliography : *A Bibliography of Writings on and by S R Ranganathan/*by A.K.Dasgupta 012 R196 D (Here D is for Das Gupta)

Sources of Research on Ranganathan/by M.P.Satija 012 R196S

Literary works

However, a difficulty arises in assigning author marks in classes where host and associated books are to be collocated especially in the class of creative literature. This need is more pronounced when a classification scheme such as the DDC does not provide individual class numbers even for prolific and major authors such as Thomas Hardy, Charles Dickens, Rabindranath Tagore or Munshi Prem Chand. Elaborate rules exist for book numbering to collocate the works on and by a prolific literary writer: to bring together all the editions of a given work, and collocate critical and translated works with the original text. For this purpose, item number/work mark is essentially required. The work number, usually consisting of the initial of the first word (excluding the definite or indefinite article) in the title, follows the author number.

822.8 W672L Wilde, Oscar: Lady Windermere's Fan

Here L has been taken from the word "Lady" in the title. It is known as work or item number. It helps to distinguish one work of the author from another and will also file them in alphabetical order. For example, the following works of Aldous Huxley in class 823.9 will get the following author and work numbers:

Antic Hay	Crome Yellow	Those Barren Leaves
H986A	H986C	H986T

Hence all the fiction works of Huxley will get arranged alphabetically by title.

In case two works of a literary author begin with the same initial letter then one of them may be distinguished by using two initial letters to keep the works in alphabetical order;

Gaban by Munshi Premchand 891.4335 P925G

Godaan by Munshi Premchand 891.4335 P925GD (here O has not been used to avoid confusion with 0). Similarly,

Ghare Baire by Gurudev Rabindranath Tagore 891.4434 T128G

Gora by Rabindranath Tagore 891.4434 T128GR

Keeping the Host and the Associated Books Together

The most difficult role for book/work numbers is in the case of prolific and much written about writers, especially for the translations, critical evaluation and commentaries on literary works of an author. Here work numbers not only have to bring the host and associated books together, but also to file them in a logical order. Donald J. Lehnus (1980, 96-97) recommends the following order:

1. Complete works

2. Selected works
3. Individual works; their translations and commentaries
4. Writings related with collective works, such as bibliographies, concordances, quotations
5. Biographies, autobiographies, letters, etc.
6. General evaluation of the work of the author

To effect this desired arrangement, the work number usually consists of two or more digits or sometimes no digit at all.

Complete Works

Do not assign any work number to any compilation of the complete works of the author; the Cutter number for the author is followed by a second cutter number for the editor/compiler. For example, Alexander Pope, *Poetical Works*, edited by H. Davis, will get the call number 821.5 P825 D262 Here D262 is for Davis. Let us take a few more examples:

Complete Poems of Tagore's Gitanjali by S.K. Paul 891.4414 T128 P324 (P324 for S. K. Paul)

The Essential Tagore, edited by Fakrul Alam and Radha Chakravarty 891.4434 T128 A318

Rabindranath Tagore's Complete Fictional Works 891.4434 T128

But in case a compiler, name of any editor/publisher is given it may be used as the second cutter number.

Tagore's complete Fictional works, edited by Prof. S. K. Chaudhary 891.4434 T128 C496 (here C496 is for S. K. Chaudhary)

Complete Works of Geoffrey Chaucer edited by F. W. Robinson 821.1 C496 R659 (here R659 is for Robinson).

Selected Writings

Such works include selective writings, quotations, etc. from the same author. To keep them immediately after the complete works (which usually do not have any work number) put A after the cutter number,

Last Poems of Tagore 891.4415 T128 A

Selected Poems of Tagore by the Oxford University Press 891.4415 T128AX (here X is for Oxford).

In this way the selections will get arranged by compiler/editor, and will follow the complete works.

Individual Works

Individual works of an author are arranged alphabetically by title using the initial of the title :

Rape of the Lock by Alexander Pope 821.5 P825R

Gora: A novel by Rabindranath Tagore 891.4434 T128G

Tagore's *Dak Ghar* 891.4434 T128D

Since A has already been reserved for selected works then any title beginning with A will be denoted by two initial letters, e.g.,

Apple Cart by George B. Shaw	822.9 S534AP
Arms and the Man by George B. Shaw	822.9 S534AR
Antony and Cleopatra by George B. Shaw	822.9 S534AN
But, Saint Jones by George B. Shaw	822.9 S534S

Biographies, Autobiographies, Memoirs, Letters Diaries, etc. of an Individual Author.

Digit pair ZY may reserved for such biographical materials.

A Biography of Richard Wright by Constance Webb 813.52 W952ZY W

(W is for Webb)

Richard Wright by Milton Rickles and Patricia Rickles 813.52 W952 ZY R (R is for Rickles)

But autobiographies, letters, etc. are given a letter A

Letters from a Sojourner in Europel by Rabindranath Tagore

891.44 T128ZY A

My childhood and Youth by Richard Wright 813.52 W952 ZY A.

In this way the autobiographies will file before the biographies of the same literary person.

Individual Titles Beginning with the letter X, Y or Z

Since X,Y and Z have been reserved for critical, translated, reference and other associative works respectively then in case any literary title begins with these letters then it may be denoted by two digits WA/W W, e.g.,

Zoo: an American novel (2012) by James Patterson and Michael Ledwidge may get the call number 813.54 P317WP (The number is not mnemonic with Z but will file his works in alphabetical sequence). Similarly,

Yellow (2016) by Megan Jacobson (treating it as British fiction) 823.92 J17WJ

Bibliographies, Dictionaries and Concordances. etc. on an Individual Author.

The digit pair ZX is reserved for bibliographical works on the author, and also for the dictionaries and concordances.

Jane Austin : A Critical Bibliography by R. W. Chapman 823.7 A933ZXC (here C is for Chapman)

A Concordance to the Poems of Emily Dickinson by Rosenbaum 811.4 D553ZXR

Encyclopaedia of Rabindranath Tagore by Dr. D. Basu 891.44 T128ZX B (here B is for Basu).

Usually the digit pair ZZ is reserved the critical and evaluative works on the author in general. This is followed by the initial of the critic author. For example, *An Introduction to Pope* by Pat Rogers (London, 1975) will get the call numbers

821.5 P825ZZ R

Here R is for Rogers, the author of the book.

Critical Appreciation and Translations of Individual Works of an Author

In case of critical appreciation of an individual work the digit Z follows the work number which in turn is followed by the critic-author's initial. For example, *Pope: Rape of the Lock*: *A critical study* by J. S. Cunningham (London, 1961) will get the call number 821.5 P825 RZC where R is from Rape... and C is from Cunningham. It will bring together all the commentaries on this specific work and file them alphabetically by their critic-authors.

Translations

Tagore's *Post Office*, translated by D. Mukerjee 891.4435 T128DXM (here D stands for the original title DakGhar, X for translations and M for Mukerjee). Translations of a single work can either be collocated by language, or by the translator or by both. Let us bring together the various translations of the above work by language:

Tagore's *Post Office*, translated by D. Mukerjee 891.4435 T128DXE

Tagore's DakGhar in Punjabi 891.4435 T128DXP

Tagore's DakGhar in Hindi 891.4435 T128DXH,

(here E, P, and H stand for the English, Punjabi and Hindi respectively). The two different translations of the post office in English may be further distinguished by the translator:

Tagore's *Post Office*, translated by D. Mukerjee 891.4435 T128DXEM

Tagore's *Post Office* , translated by A. Chakravarty 891.4435 T128DXEC

Here D is for the original title DakGhar. So all the translations of the *DakGhar* will file together by language of translation.

Take a Few Non-literary Works

The Das Kapital by Karl Marx 335.4 M392D. A commentary on The Das Kapital by David Ramsey will get the call number 335.4 M392DZR.

This will bring together all the books on *Das Kapital.*

Professor Krishan Kumar's Critical Commentary on Ranganarhan's *Prolegomena to library classification* 025.43 R196PZK (Here K is for Krishan)

Thus collected works will follow all the individual works and their commentaries, but precede the critical appreciation of the individual author as a whole. It is, however, an intricate technique requiring finer adjustment to ensure that no two book numbers are identical within a given class. **Local adjustments will have to be made here and there, so no rule applies irrevocably except that of local convenience**. It naturally provoked Anna C. Laws (1917, 18), an early scholar of book numbers, to say of author notation "as a system of rules to be judiciously broken"

Collective Biographies

In 1893, C. R Olin, Librarian of Butchell College (now University of Akron) devised a table to supplement Cutter's two-figure author table for arranging collective biographies. According to this table collective biographies are arranged by editor/compiler preceded the individual biographies arranged by the name of the biographee that is the subject. He used the letter A followed by numbers 11 to 99 to denote all names of editors and compilers of collective biographies. An extract from the table is given below:

A	11	Ga	35	Y 98
Ba	12	H	44	
Ch	17	I	45	Z 99
Da	25	Na	64	
Ea	28	Th	87	

Author numbers for the following editors are given against them as examples:

Adams	A 11	Thomas	A 87
Baker	A 12	Webster	A 94
Chambers	A 17	Young	A 98
Nanda	A64	Zimmerman	A99

Great American Mathematicians by Thomas Young B/510.92 A98

To distinguish biographies of persons whose surnames begin with A from the collective biographies, all individual biographies of persons whose surname starts with

A began with the first two initial letters followed by a number from Cutter's two figure author table. For example, a biography of Arnold will be Ar 6. *Webster's biographical dictionary* will have A94 as book number, while Biography of Hans Christian Anderson will have the book number An2. For the rest of the problems, Cutter two-figure tables rules were used as such. The Olin table remained appended to the Dewey Decimal Classification from edition 7 to 11 (1911-1932).

Notes

Original tables

C.A. Cutter's Alphabetic Order Tables-Consonants Except S. Altered and Fitted with Three-Figures, by Kate E. Sanborn, Library Bureau, Boston, 1895, 14pp of Tables, 33x28 cm

C.A. Cutter's Alphabetic Order Table. Alternatives for the Vowels and S. Altered and Fitted with Three Figures, by Kate E. Sanborn, Library Bureau, Boston, 1892.4pp of Tables, 33x17 cm.

C.A. Cutter's Alphabetic Order Table Consonants Except S and Vowels and S. Altered and Fitted with Three Figures, by Kate E. Sanborn, Library Bureau, Boston, 1896, 18pp of Tables, 13x15 cm.

Modern reprints

C A. Cutter's Two Figure Author Table, Swanson-Swift Revision 1969, H.R. Huntting Co., Chicopee, MA, 1969, 29 pp, 39x29 cm.

C. A. Cutter's Three Figure Author Table, Swanson-Swift Revision 1969, H.R. Huntting Co., Chicopee, MA, 1969, 29 pp, 39x29 cm.

Cutter-Sanborn Three Figure Author Table, Swanson-Swift Revision 1969, H.R. Huntting Co., Chicopee, MA, 1969, 33 pp, 39x22 cm.

Cutter-Sanborn Three Figure Author Table, Huntting Co., Chicopee, MA (Distributors), 1964, 8 pp, 35 cm.

References

Barden, Bertha R. (1937) *Book Numbers: A Manual for students with a Basic Code of Rules*, American Library Association, Chicago, p.7.

Carter, Ruth C. (1970) "Shelflist" In *Encyclopedia of library and information science/* ed. by Allen Kent, *et al*. New York: Marcel Dekker,Vol.27, pp.332-336

Comaromi, John P. (1981) *Book Numbers: A Historical Study and Practical Guide to their Use.* Libraries Unlimited, Littleton, CO, p. 118

Chan, Lois Mai (1994). *Cataloging and Classification: An Introduction*, 2nded. New York: Mcgraw-Hill,pp.11-12.

Denton, William (Feb2003) "Book Numbers" htttp://www.miskatonic.org/library/book- numbers.html(Accessed on 10 March, 2020)

Dewey, Melvil (1885). *Decimal classification and relative index*,2nded. Boston:Library Bureau, pp.35-37.

Laws, A.C.(1917). *Author Notation in the Library of Congress*, Washington, D.C.: Government Printing Office, p. 18.

Lehnus, D. J. (1980) *Book Numbers: History, Principles, and Application*, Chicago: American Library Association, pp. 58-66.

Olin, C. R. (1893) "An Order Table for Collective Biography," *Libr. J.*, 18, 144 (May 1893).

O'Neill, Edward T. *et al*,(1996) "Four-Figure Cutter Tables", p. 4. http://digitalarchive.oclc.org/da/ViewObjectMain.jsp?objid= 0000003355&frame=true. (Accessed on 10 March 2020).

Satija, M. P.(1987). "History of Book Numbers," *Int. Classif.,* 14(2), Sec 6 This paper also explains some Indian cuttering procedures; and catalogues some unauthorized editions of Cutter-Sanborn tables published in India.

Satija, M.P. (2008). *Book Numbers:Indian and Cutter*. New Delhi: Viva Books,xi,132p.

Savic, Dobrica (1996) "Cutt-x: An Expert System for Automatic assignment of cutter numbers", *Cat &Classif* Qly 22(2), 71-87.

Additional Readings

Aida Slavic "Call numbers and book numbers and collection arrangements in the European library traditions" In: Jagtar Singh, I.V. Malhan and Trishanjit Kaur, Eds. *Library and Information Science in Digital Age*. New Delhi: Ess Ess, 2009, vol. 1,pp.257-285.

M.P. Satija, "Book number and call number" In *Encyclopedia of library and information science/* ed. by Allen Kent, *et al*. New York: Marcel Dekker, Vol.45, 1990, pp.18-45.

A.G. Taylor, "Creation of complete call numbers." In her *Introduction to cataloguing and classification*. 10th ed. Westport,CT: Libraries Unlimited, 2006. p. 448-455.

Index to Chapters 1 to 3

Bibliography and references have not been indexed. All the entries are in context of book numbers and shelf listing.

4

Supplemented Cutter–Sanborn Author Table

Introduction

Every author number uniformly begins with one letter followed by a decimal digit varying from one to three: two digits for the letters E, I, O, J, K, Y, and Z; one digit for letters Q and X; all other letters use three decimal digits. Original table had 12361 entries. This extended table has approximately 15850 entries.

The table has been supplemented with Indian names. It may be made clear here that it is not any new table for Indian names, but only provides readymade cutter numbers for them as the librarians would have assigned them using the standard table. New names have been added at their alphabetical place for the librarians to readily use the table. It is a time saver. Personal and family names of all communities from all the regions have been taken from various library catalogues and books-in-prints. It also includes some corporate names and words likely to form a heading in library cataloguing. Some Western names have also been added in a row to facilitate Indian cataloguers.

How to Use the Table

To assign a Cutter number, determine the first word of the heading (it could be a place name, personal or corporate name, or the title of the document) and locate the number corresponding to it in the table under that alphabet. When a number has been found, it is to be preceded by the initial letter of the heading. This will be the Cutter number—first and primary part of the book number. For example, John Abbott will have the Cutter number A 127. But more often than not there will be no number to fit the name heading congruently. In that case, the closest approximation to that number will be taken, for example, Maxwell will be M 465, and Macbeth M 118. Usually, a heading will fall between two words in the table, in such a case the lower number of the two is to be assigned. For example, a name Peh, which has not been enumerated, falls between Peg 376 and Pei 377, will be denoted by P376. Similarly a cutter number for any word or combination of letters may be assigned.

A

Aa	111	Abd	135	Abraham	159
Aaan	112	Abdul	136	Abrai	161
Aal	112	Abdullah	136	Abrar	159
Aamer	112	Abdy	137	Abre	162
Aar	113	Abe	138	Abri	163
Aars	114	Abel	139	Abrol	163
Aas	115	Abel, L.	141	Abru	164
Aatre	115	Aben	142	Abu	165
Aba	116	Aber	143	Abul	166
Abad	116	Abercr	144	Abur	167
Abal	117	Aberd	145	Aca	168
Abar	118	Abern	146	Academy	168
Abat	119	Abert	147	Acc	169
Abau	121	Abha	147	Acci	171
Abb	122	Abhedananda	147	Acco	172
Abbas	122	Abhimanyu	147	Ace	173
Abbase	122	Abhinav	147	Aces	174
Abbat	123	Abhiyankear	147	Ach	175
Abbe	124	Abi	148	Achar	176
Abbey	124	Abid	148	Achars	176
Abbi	124	Abing	149	Acharya	176
Abbo	125	Abk	151	Ache	177
Abbot	126	Abl	152	Achi	178
Abbot, J.	127	Able	152	Achm	179
Abbot, M	128	Abn	153	Achut	179
Abbot, S.	129	Abo	154	Aci	181
Abbott	131	Abou	155	Ack	182
Abbott, J.	132	About	156	Acko	182
Abbott, M.	133	Abov	157	Ackw	183
Abbott, S.	134	Abr	158	Acl	184
		Abrah	159	Aco	185

Acq	186
Acr	187
Acres	187
Act	188
Action	188
Acu	189
Ada	191
Ada	191
Adal	192
Adam	193
Adam	193
Adam, J.	194
Adam, M.	195
Adam, S.	196
Adam, W.	197
Adami	198
Adamo	199
Adams	211
Adams, F.	212
Adams, G.	213
Adams, J.	214
Adams, M.	215
Adams, N.	216
Adams, S.	217
Adams, T.	218
Adams, W.	219
Adamson	221
Adani	221
Adarkar	221
Adarsh	221
Add	222
Adde	223
Addi	224
Addison	225
Addison, M.	226
Addison, S.	227
Ade	228
Adel	228
Adelh	229
Adelo	231
Aden	232
Aden	232
Adet	233
Adh	234
Adhikari	234
Adi	235
Adi Granth	235
Adi Shankra	235
Adil	235
Adinarayan	235
Adiseshiah	235
Aditi	235
Aditya	235
Adk	236
Adl	237
Adlakha	237
Adler	237
Adm	238
Administration	238
Ado	239
Ador	241
Adr	242
Adri	243
Ads	244
Advance	244
Advani	244
Ady	245
Adyar	245
Ae	246
Aeg	247
Ael	248
Aem	249
Aen	251
Aer	252
Aes	253
Aeso	254
Aet	255
Afa	256
Affl	257
Afr	258
African	258
Afsar	258
Afzal	258
Aga	259
Agar	261
Agarwal	261
Agas	262
Agat	263
Agay	264
Age	265
Agesthialingam	265
Agg	266
Agha	266

Agi	267	Aik	291	Akhtar	315
Agis	268	Aiki	292	Al	316
Agl	269	Ail	293	Alagh	316
Agn	271	Aim	294	Alain	317
Agnes	272	Aima	294	Alain	318
Agnew	273	Ain	295	Alam	318
Agnihotri	273	Ains	296	Alam	319
Agno	274	Ainsw	297	Alan	319
Ago	275	Ainsworht	297	Alar	321
Agou	276	Air	298	Alard	322
Agr	277	Airan	298	Alary	323
Agri	278	Ais	299	Alav	324
Agriculture	278	Ait	311	Alb	325
Agrip	279	Aitken	311	Alban	326
Agro	281	Aiyar	311	Albar	327
Agu	282	Aiyenger	311	Albe	328
Aguil	283	Aj	312	Alber	329
Aguir	284	Aj	313	Albri	342
Agwani	284	Ajantha	312	Albriz	343
Ah	285	Ajay	312	Albro	344
Ahir	285	Ajit	312	Albu	345
Ahlawat	285	Ajwani	312	Alc	346
Ahluwalia	285	Ak	313	Alcan	347
Ahm	286	Akal	314	Alcar	348
Ahmad	286	Akbar	314	Alcaz	349
Ahmed	286	Aker	314	Alce	351
Ahr	287	Aker	315	Alci	352
Ahsan	287	Akers	315	Alcip	353
Ahuja	287	Akers	316	Alco	354
Ai	288	Akhil	315	Alcot	355
Aig	289			Alcu	356

Ald	357
Alden	358
Alden, S.	359
Alder	361
Alders	362
Aldi	363
Aldo	364
Aldr	365
Ale	366
Alem	367
Alen	368
Alep	369
Ales	371
Alessi	372
Alew	373
Alex	374
Alexander, C.	375
Alexander, J.	376
Alexander, M.	377
Alexander, S.	378
Alexander, W.	379
Alexandre	381
Alexandre, M.	382
Alexandro	383
Alexi	384
Alfa	385
Alfe	386
Alfi	387
Alfo	388
Alford	389
Alfr	391
Alfred	392
Alfri	393
Alg	394
Alger	395
Algh	396
Alh	397
Alha	415
Ali	398
Alif	399
Alig	411
Alip	412
Alis	413
Alison, M.	414
Alk	415
All	416
Allah	416
Allan	417
Allan, M.	418
Allard	419
Allas	421
Alle	422
Allein	423
Allem	424
Allen	425
Allen, J.	427
Allen, N.	428
Allen, S.	429
Allen, T.	431
Allen, W.	432
Allens	433
Aller	434
Alley	435
Alli	436
Alling	437
Allis	438
Allison, M.	439
Allo	441
Alls	442
Ally	443
Alm	444
Alman	445
Almas	446
Alme	447
Almen	448
Almi	449
Almo	451
Almon	452
Alo	453
Alok	453
Alon	454
Alos	455
Alp	456
Alpi	457
Alq	458
Alr	459
Als	461
Alsop	462
Alste	463
Alsto	464
Alt	465
Altbach	465
Alte	466

Altekar	466
Alter	466
Alterkar	466
Alth	467
Alti	468
Alto	469
Alu	471
Alv	472
Alva	472
Alvare	473
Alve	474
Alvi	475
Alvo	476
Alw	477
Alz	478
Alzhe	478
Ama	479
Amad	481
Amal	482
Amalt	483
Aman	484
Amar	485
Amas	486
Amat	487
Amato	488
Amau	489
Amazon	489
Amb	491
Ambani	491
Ambedkar	491
Ambi	492
Ambl	493
Ambo	494
Ambr	495
Ambros	496
Ambu	497
Ambuja	497
Ame	498
Ameer	498
Amelo	499
Amen	511
Amer	512
American	512
Ames	513
Ames, M.	514
Amh	515
Ami	516
Amin	517
Amir	517
Amm	518
Ammir	519
Ammo	521
Amn	522
Amo	523
Amor	524
Amos	525
Amp	526
Amps	527
Amrik	527
Amrit	527
Amritsar	527
Ams	528
Amu	529
Amul	529
Amy	531
Ana	532
Anam	533
Anand	533
Anant	533
Anas	534
Anat	535
Anax	536
Anb	537
Anc	538
Anch	539
Anci	541
Anco	542
And	543
Andeman	543
Anders	544
Anderson	545
Anderson, D.	546
Anderson, J.	547
Anderson, M.	548
Anderson, R.	549
Anderson, T.	551
Anderson, W.	552
Andhra	552
Andley	552
Andr	553
Andral	554
Andre	555
Andrea	556

Andreas	557
Andree	558
Andrei	559
Andres	561
Andrew	562
Andrew, M.	563
Andrewe	564
Andrews	565
Andrews, E.	566
Andrews, J.	567
Andrews, M.	568
Andrews, S.	569
Andrews, T.	571
Andrews, W.	572
Andri	573
Andro	574
Andron	575
Andros	576
Andry	577
Ane	578
Aneja	578
Aner	579
Ang	581
Angeli	582
Angell	583
Angelo	584
Angelu	585
Angen	586
Anger	587
Angi	588
Angl	589
Anglu	591
Ango	592
Angou	593
Angu	594
Angus	595
Anh	596
Ani	597
Anil	597
Anim	598
Anirudh	598
Anis	599
Anita	599
Anjali	599
Anjaneyulu	599
Anjli	599
Anju	599
Anjwala	599
Ank	611
Anl	612
Ann	613
Annapurna	613
Annes	614
Anni	615
Anq	616
Anreja	616
Ans	617
Ansal	617
Ansari	617
Ansel	618
Ansi	619
Ansl	621
Anso	622
Ansp	623
Anst	624
Anstey	625
Ansti	626
Ant	627
Antho	628
Anthony	628
Anti	629
Antim	631
Antio	632
Antip	633
Anto	634
Antoni	635
Antony	635
Antr	636
Anup	636
Anuradha	636
Anv	637
Ao	638
Ap	639
Apache	639
Aparajit	639
Apel	641
Api	642
Apo	643
Apollo	644
Apos	645
App	646
Appa	646
Appadosai	646

Appi	647
Appl	648
Appleton	649
Appleton, J.	651
Appleton, T.	652
Appu	653
Apr	654
Apt	655
Apte	655
Apurva	655
Aqu	656
Aquin	657
Ara	658
Ara	658
Arag	659
Aram	661
Aran	662
Arat	663
Arati	663
Arb	664
Arbi	664
Arbl	665
Arbo	666
Arbu	667
Arc	668
Arch	669
Archer	671
Archer, M.	672
Archi	673
Arci	674
Arco	675
Arcot	675
Ard	676
Ardo	677
Are	678
Areh	679
Aren	681
Aret	682
Aretin	683
Arex	684
Arf	685
Arg	686
Argel	687
Argen	688
Argent	689
Argenti	691
Argi	692
Argo	693
Argu	694
Argy	695
Ari	696
Arib	697
Arid	698
Arif	698
Arig	699
Arin	711
Ario	712
Arip	713
Aris	714
Aristi	715
Aristo	716
Aristop	717
Aristotle	717
Ariu	718
Ariz	719
Arjan	719
Arjun	721
Ark	721
Arkw	722
Arl	723
Arling	724
Arlo	725
Arlu	726
Arm	727
Arme	728
Armi	729
Armis	731
Armit	732
Armitage, M.	733
Arms	734
Armstrong	735
Armstrong, J.	736
Armstrong, M.	737
Armstrong, S.	738
Armstrong, W.	739
Army	741
Arn	742
Arnal	743
Arnau	744
Arnaul	745
Arnay	746
Arnd	747
Arne	748

Arneja	748
Arni	749
Arno	751
Arnold	752
Arnold, D.	753
Arnold, G.	754
Arnold, H.	755
Arnold, J.	756
Arnold, M.	757
Arnold, R.	758
Arnold, T.	759
Arnold, W.	761
Arnoldi	762
Arnon	763
Arnot	764
Arnou	765
Arnoult	766
Arns	767
Arnu	768
Aro	769
Arora	769
Arou	771
Arp	772
Arr	773
Arre	774
Arri	775
Arrig	776
Arriv	777
Arro	778
Arrows	779
Ars	781
Arsi	782
Arsl	783
Art	784
Art	784
Artau	785
Arte	786
Arth	787
Arther	787
Arthur	788
Arthur, M.	789
Arthur, S.	791
Arto	792
Aru	793
Arun	793
Arunachal	793
Arunachalam	793
Arundale	793
Arunima	793
Arunt	794
Arv	795
Arvind	795
Arw	796
Arya	796
Aryan	796
Arz	797
Asa	798
Asad	798
Asadullah	798
Asaf	798
Asb	799
Asc	811
Asch	812
Aschen	813
Ascl	814
Asco	815
Ase	816
Asf	817
Asg	818
Ash	819
Ashat	819
Ashbu	821
Ashburt	822
Ashby	823
Ashe	824
Asher	825
Ashfaq	825
Ashk	825
Ashl	826
Ashm	827
Ashok	827
Ashraf	827
Asht	828
Ashton, M.	829
Ashu	829
Ashw	831
Asi	832
Asia	832
Asif	832
Asija	832
Asio	833
Ask	834
Askari	834

Askew	835	Asundi	861	Atti	885
Aslam	835	Ata	862	Attw	886
Asm	836	Atal	862	Atul	886
Aso	837	Atam	862	Atw	887
Asopa	837	Atar	862	Atwal	887
Asp	838	Atch	863	Au	887
Asper	839	Ate	864	Aub	888
Aspi	841	Ath	865	Aubert	889
Aspl	842	Athalye	865	Aubery	891
Aspr	843	Athe	866	Aubes	892
Asrani	843	Athen	867	Aubi	893
Ass	844	Ather	868	Aubin	894
Assam	844	Atherton	869	Aubr	895
Assange	844	Athi	871	Aubry	896
Assen	845	Ati	872	Aubu	897
Asser	846	Atk	873	Auc	898
Assh	847	Atkins	874	Auckland	898
Assi	848	Atkins, M.	874	Aud	899
Asso	849	Atkinson	875	Audi	911
Association	849	Atkinson, J.	876	Audin	912
Assu	851	Atkinson, M.	877	Audl	913
Ast	852	Atkinson, T.	878	Audo	914
Aste	853	Atky	879	Audr	915
Asthana	853	Atl	881	Audu	916
Asti	854	Atma	881	Audux	916
Astl	855	Atr	882	Aue	917
Asto	856	Atri	882	Auf	918
Aston	857	Att	883	Aug	919
Astor	858	Attar	883	Augi	921
Astr	859	Attenbrough	883	Augu	922
Asu	861	Atter	884	Augus	923

Augutine	923	Avasthi	946	Ayd	975
Aul	924	Avau	947	Aye	976
Aulakh	924	Ave	948	Ayer	976
Aullucke	924	Avell	949	Ayers	977
Aum	925	Aven	951	Ayl	978
Aun	926	Aver	952	Aylm	979
Aur	927	Avero	953	Aylw	981
Aurbindo	927	Avery	954	Aym	982
Auri	928	Avery, M.	955	Ayn	983
Auriv	929	Avez	956	Ayr	984
Aurl	928	Avi	957	Ayres	985
Aurng	929	Avila	958	Ayrt	986
Auro	931	Avinash	958	Ays	987
Aurora	931	Avit	958	Ayt	988
Aus	932	Avit	959	Ayton	989
Austen	933	Avo	961	Ayub	989
Austen, M.	934	Avos	962	Ayurveda	989
Austin	935	Avr	963	Ayush	989
Austin, J.	936	Avtar	963	Ayyanger	989
Austin, M.	937	Awa	964	Ayyar	989
Austin, T.	938	Awasthi	964	Ayyub	989
Australia	938	Awb	965	Aza	991
Aut	939	Awd	966	Azad	991
Autr	941	Awi	967	Azami	991
Auv	942	Ax	968	Azar	992
Aux	943	Axel	969	Aze	993
Auz	944	Axo	971	Azev	994
Ava	945	Axt	972	Azi	995
Avadhane	945	Aya	973	Aziz	995
Avalon	945	Ayan	973	Azo	996
Avan	946	Ayc	974	Azr	997

Azvita	997
Azy	998
Azz	999

B

Ba	111
Baar	111
Bab	112
Baba	112
Babar	112
Babbar	112
Babe	113
Babi	114
Baboo	114
Babr	115
Babu	115
Baby	115
Bac	116
Bacci	117
Bach	118
Bachan	118
Bache	119
Bachell	121
Bachet	122
Bachi	123
Bachm	124
Baci	125
Back	126
Bacm	127
Baco	128
Bacon, M.	129
Bacon,F	128
Bacr	131
Bad	132
Badal	132
Badami	132
Badan	132
Bade	133
Baden	134
Badg	135
Badh	135
Badi	136
Bado	137
Badr	138
Bae	139
Baer	141
Baert	142
Baf	143
Bag	144
Bagavathi	144
Bagchi	144
Bagga	144
Baghi	145
Bagi	145
Bagl	146
Bagley	146
Bagn	147
Bago	148
Bags	149
Bah	151
Bahadur	151
Bahri	151
Bahuguna	151
Bai	152
Baidya	152
Baig	152
Baij	152
Bail	153
Baile	154
Bailey, L.	155
Bailey, S.	156
Baill	157
Baillo	158
Bails	159
Baily	161
Bain	162
Baini	162
Bains	162
Bair	163
Baisya	163
Bait	164
Baj	165
Bajaj	165
Bajpai	165
Bajracharya	165
Bajwa	165
Bak	166
Bake	167
Baker	168
Baker, M.	168
Bakewell	168
Bakht	168
Baks	169
Bakshi	169

Bakya	166
Bal	171
Bala	171
Balachandran	171
Balakrishna	171
Balan	171
Balasubr	171
Balb	172
Balbir	172
Balbo	173
Balc	174
Balchandani	174
Bald	175
Balder	176
Baldev	176
Baldi	177
Baldo	178
Baldu	179
Baldw	181
Baldwin, M.	182
Bale	183
Baler	184
Baleri	185
Bales	184
Balf	185
Balgopal	185
Bali	186
Baljit	186
Ball	187
Balla	188
Ballar	189
Balle	191
Balli	192
Ballo	193
Balm	194
Balo	195
Balraj	195
Balram	195
Bals	196
Balt	197
Balu	198
Balwant	198
Bam	199
Bamp	211
Bamzai	211
Ban	212
Banabhatta	212
Banc	213
Band	214
Bandhopadhya	214
Bandhyopadhyay	214
Bandra	214
Bane	215
Banerjea	215
Banerjee	215
Banerji	215
Bang	216
Banga	216
Bangalore	216
Bangladesh	216
Bani	217
Bank	218
Bann	219
Bansal	219
Bansthali	219
Banu	219
Banwari	219
Bao	221
Bap	222
Bapat	222
Bapna	222
Bapu	222
Bar	223
Baradol	223
Barag	224
Baral	224
Baran	225
Barat	226
Barau	227
Barb	228
Barbar	229
Barbat	231
Barbau	232
Barbe	233
Barber	234
Barbet	235
Barbi	236
Barbil	237
Barbo	238
Barbou	239
Barbu	241
Barc	242
Barch	243

Barcl	244	Barre	271	Base	299
Bard	245	Barreh	271	Basham	299
Barden	245	Barrer	272	Basi	311
Bardhan	245	Barret	273	Basili	312
Bardi	246	Barrett	274	Basin	313
Bardo	247	Barri	275	Basir	314
Bare	248	Barrier	275	Bask	315
Barf	249	Barrin	276	Basm	316
Barg	251	Barro	277	Bass	317
Bari	252	Barrow	278	Basse	318
Barik	252	Barry	279	Basset	319
Barin	253	Barry, L.	281	Bassi	321
Bark	254	Bars	282	Basso	322
Barker	255	Bart	283	Bassu	323
Barki	256	Barth	284	Bast	324
Barl	257	Barthel	285	Baste	325
Barlo	258	Bartho	286	Basti	326
Barman	258	Bartholo	287	Basto	327
Barn	259	Bartholonew	287	Basu	327
Barnala	259	Barti	288	Bat	328
Barnes	261	Bartl	289	Bates	329
Barnh	262	Bartlett, M.	291	Bath	331
Barnu	263	Barto	292	Bathu	332
Baro	264	Barton	293	Bati	333
Baron	265	Bartr	294	Batliboi	333
Baron	267	Baru	295	Bato	334
Baroni	266	Barua	295	Batra	334
Barooah	266	Barw	296	Batt	335
Barot	267	Bas	297	Batti	336
Barr	268	Basak	297	Bau	337
Barras	269	Basc	298	Baud	338

Baudio	339	Be	365	Becky	397
Baudo	341	Beal	366	Becm	398
Baudr	342	Bean	367	Bed	399
Baudu	343	Bear	368	Bede	411
Baue	344	Beas	368	Bedi	412
Bauf	345	Beat	369	Bedr	413
Baug	346	Beau	371	Bee	414
Baum	347	Beauch	372	Beer	415
Baumg	348	Beaucl	373	Beg	416
Baun	349	Beauf	374	Begi	417
Baur	351	Beaug	375	Begu	418
Baut	352	Beauh	376	Begum	418
Bav	353	Beaul	377	Beh	419
Bava	353	Beaum	378	Behl	419
Bavakutty	353	Beaumo	379	Behr	421
Baveja	353	Beaun	381	Behra	421
Bavi	354	Beaup	382	Bei	422
Bawa	354	Beaur	383	Beis	423
Baweja	354	Beaus	384	Bek	424
Bawra	354	Beauv	385	Bel	425
Bax	355	Beauvo	386	Belan	426
Baxi	355	Beb	387	Belch	427
Bay	356	Bec	388	Bele	428
Baye	357	Bece	389	Belg	429
Bayl	358	Bech	391	Beli	431
Bayly	359	Bechs	392	Belk	432
Bayn	361	Beck	393	Bell	433
Baz	362	Becke	394	Bell, L.	434
Bazaz	362	Becker	395	Bell, R.	435
Bazi	363	Becker, P.	396	Bellan	436
Bazo	364	Becki	397	Bellav	437

Belle	438	Beni	467	Bergi	498
Belleg	439	Beniwal	467	Bergm	499
Bellen	441	Benj	468	Berh	499
Beller	442	Benjamin	468	Beri	511
Belli	443	Benn	469	Berk	512
Bellin	444	Bennett	471	Berkl	513
Bellm	445	Bennett, M.	472	Berl	514
Bello	446	Beno	473	Berlia	514
Bellon	447	Bens	474	Berlin	515
Bellow	448	Bent	475	Berm	516
Bellu	449	Benth	476	Bern	517
Belm	451	Bentl	477	Bernar	518
Belo	452	Bentley	477	Bernard, J.	519
Belt	453	Bento	478	Bernard, M.	521
Belv	454	Benw	479	Bernard, T.	522
Bely	454	Beo	481	Bernardi	523
Bem	455	Bepin	481	Bernat	524
Ben	456	Ber	482	Berne	525
Benc	457	Berar	483	Bernet	526
Bend	458	Berau	484	Bernh	527
Bendo	459	Berc	485	Berni	528
Bendre	459	Berck	486	Bernier	528
Bene	461	Bere	487	Berno	529
Benede	462	Beren	488	Berns	531
Benedi	463	Berens	489	Bero	532
Benef	464	Beres	491	Berr	533
Benegal	464	Beret	492	Berry	534
Benel	465	Berg	493	Bers	535
Beng	466	Bergan	494	Bert	536
Bengal	466	Berge	495	Berte	537
Bengla	466	Berger	496	Berth	538

Berthe	539	Beveridge	571	Bharti	575
Berthi	541	Bew	572	Bhartiya	575
Bertho	542	Bey	573	Bhartrihari	575
Berti	543	Bez	574	Bharucha	575
Bertin	544	Bezant	574	Bhasin	575
Berto	545	Bezos	574	Bhaskar	575
Bertol	546	Bh	575	Bhat	575
Berton	547	Bhabha	575	Bhati	575
Bertr	548	Bhadra	575	Bhatia	575
Bertrand, F.	549	Bhaduri	575	Bhatnagar	575
Bertrand, N.	551	Bhagat	575	Bhatt	575
Bertu	552	Bhagwan	575	Bhattacharya	575
Berw	553	Bhagwant	575	Bhaumick	575
Bes	554	Bhagwat	575	Bhavani	575
Besant	554	Bhai	575	Bhavon	575
Besl	555	Bhak	575	Bhende	575
Beso	556	Bhakta	575	Bhikshu	575
Bess	557	Bhalla	575	Bhimsen	575
Bessem	558	Bhambhri	575	Bhojwani	575
Bessi	559	Bhamrah	575	Bhola	575
Best	561	Bhan	575	Bhom	575
Bet	562	Bhandare	575	Bhootlingam	575
Beteille	562	Bhandari	575	Bhopal	575
Bethm	563	Bhandarkar	575	Bhowmik	575
Beto	564	Bhanja	575	Bhuk	575
Bett	565	Bhanot	575	Bhullar	575
Beu	566	Bhapat	575	Bhum	575
Beul	567	Bhardwaj	575	Bhupal	575
Beus	568	Bhargava	575	Bhupinder	575
Beut	569	Bharta	575	Bhushan	575
Bev	571	Bharthi	575	Bhutani	575

Bhutia	575	Bimal	611	Blackw	632
Bhutto	575	Bin	612	Blag	633
Bhuyan	575	Bindra	612	Blai	634
Bi	576	Bing	613	Blair	635
Bian	577	Binn	614	Blak	636
Bianco	578	Binwal	614	Blake	636
Biar	579	Bio	615	Blakes	637
Bib	581	Bior	616	Blan	638
Bibl	582	Bipan	616	Blanch	639
Bible	582	Bir	617	Blanche	641
Bic	583	Bird	618	Bland	642
Bid	584	Birg	618	Blanq	643
Bidani	584	Birk	619	Blas	644
Bide	585	Birla	619	Blau	645
Bie	586	Bis	621	Ble	646
Biel	587	Bish	622	Blen	647
Bien	588	Bishop	622	Bli	648
Bies	589	Bisht	622	Blis	649
Bif	591	Biss	623	Bliss	649
Big	592	Bist	623	Blo	651
Bigl	593	Biswa	623	Block	651
Bigo	594	Biswal	623	Blod	652
Bihar	594	Biswas	623	Blom	653
Bijlani	594	Bit	624	Blon	654
Bil	595	Biz	625	Bloo	655
Bilgrami	595	Bj	626	Blool	655
Bill	596	Bl	627	Bloom	655
Bille	597	Black	627	Bloomberg	655
Billi	598	Black, M	629	Blos	656
Billo	599	Black,B	628	Blou	657
Bim	611	Blacks	631	Blu	658

Blum	658
Blunt	659
Bly	661
Bo	662
Board	662
Bob	663
Bobby	663
Boc	664
Bock	665
Bod	666
Bodi	667
Bodl	668
Boe	669
Boeh	671
Boer	672
Boet	673
Bog	674
Bogi	675
Boh	676
Bohn	677
Bohra	677
Boi	678
Boil	679
Boin	681
Bois	682
Boisg	683
Boiss	684
Boit	685
Bok	686
Bol	687
Bole	688
Boli	689
Boll	691
Bolli	692
Bolo	693
Bolt	694
Bom	695
Bombay	695
Bombwall	695
Boml	696
Bon	697
Bonap	698
Bonar	699
Bond	711
Bone	712
Bonf	713
Bonh	714
Boni	715
Bonn	716
Bonnet	717
Bonni	718
Bono	719
Bons	721
Bont	722
Bonv	723
Boo	724
Book	724
Bool	724
Boot	725
Booth	725
Bor	726
Boral	726
Bord	727
Borden	728
Bordi	729
Bore	731
Borg	732
Borgi	733
Borgo	734
Borgohain	734
Borkar	734
Borl	735
Born	736
Borr	737
Borris	738
Bors	738
Bort	739
Bos	741
Bosch	742
Bose	743
Boso	744
Boss	745
Bossu	746
Bost	747
Bot	748
Both	749
Bott	751
Bou	752
Bouche	753
Bouchi	754
Boucho	755
Boud	756
Bouf	757

Boug	758	Boy	789	Bray	827
Bouh	759	Boyd	789	Brazil	827
Boui	761	Boye	791	Bre	828
Bouil	762	Boyl	792	Brec	829
Boul	763	Boys	793	Bred	831
Boull	764	Br	794	Bree	832
Boulton	764	Brab	795	Breg	833
Boun	765	Brac	796	Breh	834
Bour	766	Brack	797	Brei	835
Bourc	767	Brad	798	Brem	836
Bourd	768	Bradf	799	Bren	837
Bourdi	769	Bradl	811	Brenn	838
Boure	771	Brads	812	Brent	839
Bourg	772	Brag	813	Brer	841
Bourgo	773	Brahamachari	813	Bres	842
Bouri	774	Brahma	813	Bress	843
Bourn	775	Brahman	856	Bret	844
Bourr	776	Brai	814	Brett	845
Bous	777	Bram	815	Breu	846
Bout	778	Bran	816	Brew	847
Bouth	779	Brand	817	Brews	848
Bouto	781	Brandi	818	Bri	849
Bouv	782	Brando	819	Brid	851
Bov	783	Brandt	821	Bridgm	852
Bow	784	Brar	822	Brie	853
Bowdi	785	Bras	823	Brig	854
Bowe	786	Brass	823	Briggs	854
Bower	786	Brat	824	Brigh	855
Bowker	786	Brata	824	Bright	855
Bowl	787	Brau	825	Brighto	856
Bowr	788	Brav	826	Brij	856

Bril	857	Bruce, J.	887	Bucks	926
Brin	858	Bruck	888	Bud	927
Bris	859	Brue	889	Budha	927
Brist	861	Brug	891	Budhiraja	927
Brit	862	Bruh	892	Bue	928
British	862	Brum	893	Buf	929
Bro	863	Brun	894	Bug	931
Brock	864	Brunet	895	Buhler	931
Broe	865	Bruni	896	Bui	932
Brog	866	Brunn	897	Bukhari	932
Brok	867	Bruno	898	Bul	933
Broker	867	Bruns	899	Buland	933
Brom	868	Brunsw	911	Bulchandani	933
Bron	869	Brus	912	Bulg	933
Broo	871	Brut	913	Bulk	934
Brooke	872	Bruy	914	Bull	935
Brooks	873	Bry	915	Bulle	936
Bros	874	Bryant	915	Bulli	937
Brou	875	Bryc	916	Bullo	938
Brous	876	Bryce	916	Bulo	939
Brow	877	Bu	917	Bulsara	939
Brown	878	Buad	927	Bulw	941
Brown, H.	878	Buc	918	Bun	942
Brown, M.	879	Buch	918	Bunce	942
Brown, T.	881	Buche	919	Buo	943
Browne	882	Bucho	921	Buoni	944
Browne, M.	883	Buck	922	Bur	945
Browne, S.	884	Bucki	923	Burb	946
Browni	885	Buckl	924	Burc	947
Bru	886	Buckland	924	Burck	948
Bruce	887	Buckm	925	Burd	949

Burdet	951
Bure	952
Bureau	952
Burf	953
Burg	954
Burger	954
Burges	955
Burgh	956
Burgo	957
Burh	958
Burk	959
Burke	959
Burl	961
Burm	962
Burman	962
Burn	963
Burnet	964
Burney	965
Burnh	966
Burns	967
Burr	968
Burre	969
Burri	971
Burro	972
Burt	973
Burto	974
Burton	974
Bury	975
Bus	976
Busch	977
Bush	978
Bushn	979
Buss	981
Bust	982
But	983
Butalia	983
Butani	983
Buti	984
Butl	985
Butler	986
Butler, M.	986
Butler, T.	987
Butt	988
Butto	989
Bux	991
Buy	992
By	993
Byn	994
Byr	995
Byro	996
Bys	997
Byt	998
Bz	999

C

Ca	111
Cab	112
Cabas	113
Cabe	114
Cabi	115
Cabo	116
Cabr	117
Cac	118
Cach	119
Cad	121
Cade	122
Cadet	123
Cadi	124
Cado	125
Cadr	126
Cae	127
Caes	128
Caf	129
Cag	131
Cah	132
Cai	133
Cail	134
Cain	135
Cair	136
Cais	137
Caiu	138
Caj	139
Cal	141
Calan	142
Calas	143
Calc	144
Calcutta	144
Cald	145
Calde	146
Caldw	147
Caldwell	147
Cale	148
Calen	149
Calf	151

Calh	152	Cami	183	Canni	225
Cali	153	Camm	184	Canno	226
Calin	154	Camo	185	Cano	227
Calk	155	Camp	186	Cans	228
Call	156	Campbell	187	Cant	229
Calle	157	Campbell, H.	188	Canti	231
Callewaert	157	Campbell, M.	189	Canto	232
Calli	158	Campbell, S.	191	Cantr	233
Callim	159	Campbell, W.	192	Cantw	234
Callin	161	Campe	193	Canu	235
Callis	162	Campen	194	Cap	236
Callo	163	Camper	195	Cape	237
Calm	164	Campi	196	Capel	238
Calo	165	Campis	197	Capen	239
Calt	166	Campo	198	Capet	241
Calv	167	Campr	199	Capg	242
Calvert	167	Camu	211	Capi	243
Calvi	168	Can	212	Capit	244
Calvo	169	Canada	212	Capo	245
Calz	171	Canan	213	Capom	246
Cam	172	Canb	214	Capp	247
Camas	173	Canc	215	Capper	248
Camb	174	Cand	216	Cappo	249
Cambi	175	Candi	217	Capr	251
Cambo	176	Candl	218	Capre	252
Cambr	177	Cando	219	Capri	253
Cambri	178	Cane	221	Capro	254
Cambridge	178	Canf	222	Capu	255
Camd	179	Cani	223	Caq	256
Came	181	Cann	224	Car	257
Camer	182			Caraf	258

Caram	259	Caron	293	Casat	336
Caran	261	Carp	294	Case	337
Carat	262	Carpente	295	Casen	338
Carb	263	Carpenter	296	Casi	339
Carbo	264	Carpenter, L.	296	Caso	341
Carc	265	Carpenter, S.	297	Casp	342
Card	266	Carpi	298	Cass	343
Cardi	267	Carpo	299	Casse	344
Cardo	268	Carr	311	Cassi	345
Cardw	269	Carr, M.	312	Casson	345
Care	271	Carrar	313	Cast	346
Carew	272	Carre	314	Caste	347
Carey	273	Carret	315	Castel	348
Carey, H.	274	Carri	316	Casteln	349
Carey, M.	275	Carril	317	Casti	351
Carey, S.	276	Carrin	318	Castil	352
Cari	277	Carro	319	Castl	353
Carl	278	Cars	321	Casto	354
Carlet	279	Cart	322	Castr	355
Carleton	281	Carter	323	Casw	356
Carli	282	Carter, L.	324	Cat	357
Carlis	283	Carter, S.	325	Caten	359
Carlo	284	Carth	326	Cath	361
Carlt	285	Carti	327	Cathc	362
Carly	286	Carto	328	Cathe	363
Carlyle	286	Cartw	329	Catholic	363
Carm	287	Carv	331	Cati	364
Carn	288	Cary	332	Catl	358
Carne	289	Cary, M.	333	Catl	365
Carno	291	Cas	334	Cato	366
Caro	292	Casan	335	Catr	367

Catt	368	Ceo	398	Chais	435
Catto	369	Cep	399	Chaitanya	435
Cau	371	Cer	411	Chak	435
Caul	372	Cerc	412	Chakra	435
Caum	373	Cerd	413	Chal	436
Caus	374	Cere	414	Chall	437
Caut	375	Ceri	415	Chalm	438
Cav	376	Cero	416	Chalo	439
Cavall	377	Cerr	417	Chalt	441
Cave	378	Cert	418	Cham	442
Caven	379	Cerv	419	Chamber	443
Cavendish, L.	381	Ces	421	Chambers	444
Cavi	382	Ceso	422	Chambers, M.	445
Cavo	383	Cet	423	Chambo	446
Cax	384	Cev	424	Chambr	447
Caxton	384	Cey	425	Chami	448
Cay	385	Ch	426	Champ	449
Caz	386	Chabe	427	Champe	451
Ce	387	Chabo	428	Champi	452
Ceci	388	Chabr	429	Champl	453
Ced	389	Chabra	429	Chan	454
Cei	391	Chabra	531	Chancellor	454
Cel	392	Chac	431	Chanchreek	454
Cell	393	Chach	431	Chand	454
Cels	394	Chacko	431	Chander	454
Cement	394	Chad	432	Chandigarh	454
Cen	395	Chadha	432	Chandl	455
Cens	396	Chaf	433	Chandler, M.	456
Census	396	Chagla	433	Chandra	456
Cent	397	Chahal	433	Chandrashekhar	456
Central	397	Chai	434	Chandy	456

Chanl	457	Charr	485	Cheema	515
Chann	458	Chart	486	Cheiro	515
Channa	458	Chas	487	Chel	516
Chano	458	Chass	488	Chem	517
Chant	459	Chast	489	Chen	518
Chao	461	Chastil	491	Chennai	518
Chap	462	Chat	492	Chenoy	518
Chapi	463	Chath	493	Chep	519
Chapl	464	Chati	494	Cher	521
Chapm	465	Chatrapati	494	Chere	522
Chapman	466	Chatrath	494	Cherian	521
Chapman,M	466	Chatt	495	Chero	522
Chapp	467	Chatterjee	495	Cheru	523
Chapu	468	Chattopadhya	495	Ches	524
Char	469	Chaturvedi	495	Chest	525
Charade	469	Chatwal	495	Chet	526
Charak	469	Chau	496	Chetan	526
Charan	469	Chaube	496	Chetty	526
Chard	471	Chaudhuri	496	Chetwode	526
Chare	472	Chauhan	496	Chev	527
Chari	473	Chaul	497	Chevi	528
Charl	474	Chaun	498	Chevr	529
Charles	475	Chaurasia	498	Chey	531
Charles, M.	476	Chaus	499	Chhabra	531
Charles, S.	477	Chauv	511	Chhat	531
Charlet	478	Chav	512	Chhatisgarh	531
Charlo	479	Chavan	512	Chhatwal	531
Charlt	481	Chawla	512	Chhaya	531
Charm	482	Chaz	513	Chholey	531
Charn	483	Che	514	Chi	532
Charp	484	Chee	515	Chib	532

Chibber	532
Chich	533
Chidambar	533
Chidnanda	533
Chief	533
Chif	534
Chikate	534
Chil	535
Child	536
Childs	537
Chill	538
Chin	539
China	539
Chinmaya	539
Chip	541
Chis	542
Chisti	542
Chit	543
Chitale	543
Chitkara	543
Chla	544
Chls	544
Cho	545
Chohan	545
Chois	546
Chol	547
Chola	547
Chom	548
Chomasky	548
Choodamani	548
Chop	549
Chopra	549
Chor	551
Chou	552
Choubey	552
Choudhry	552
Chouhan	552
Chowdhry	552
Chr	553
Chri	554
Christ	554
Christi	555
Christo	556
Chro	557
Chry	558
Chu	559
Church	561
Church, M.	562
Churchill	563
Chut	564
Ci	565
Cian	566
Cib	567
Cic	568
Cie	569
Cig	571
Cil	572
Cim	573
Cin	574
Cini	575
Cio	576
Cip	577
Cir	578
Circus	578
Cis	579
Cit	581
Civ	582
Civil	582
Cl	583
Clag	584
Clai	585
Clam	586
Clan	587
Clap	588
Clapp	589
Clapper	589
Clar	591
Clara	591
Clark	592
Clark, G.	593
Clark, M.	594
Clark, S.	595
Clark, W.	596
Clarke	597
Clarke, G.	598
Clarke, M.	599
Clarke, S.	611
Clarke, W.	612
Clarks	613
Clary	614
Clau	615
Claus	616
Clav	617

Clax	618
Clay	619
Clay, M.	621
Clay, T.	622
Cle	623
Clee	624
Clem	625
Clement	626
Clements	626
Cleo	628
Cler	629
Clerk	631
Clerke	632
Clerm	633
Cles	634
Clev	635
Clevelend	635
Cli	636
Clif	637
Clifford	638
Clifford, M.	638
Clift	639
Clin	641
Clinton	641
Clio	641
Cliv	642
Clo	643
Clon	644
Clos	645
Clot	646
Clou	647
Clow	648
Clu	649
Cn	651
Co	652
Coats	652
Cobb	653
Cobbet	654
Cobbler	654
Cobd	655
Cobh	656
Cobo	657
Cobu	658
Coc	659
Coch	661
Cochin	662
Cochr	663
Cock	664
Cockb	665
Cocke	666
Coco	667
Cocq	668
Cod	669
Codd	669
Codm	671
Coe	672
Coes	673
Cof	674
Coffin	675
Cog	676
Cogs	677
Coh	678
Cohen	678
Coig	679
Coit	681
Cok	682
Col	683
Colb	684
Colbu	685
Colby	686
Colc	687
Cold	688
Cole	689
Coleb	691
Colem	692
Coleman	693
Coler	693
Colet	694
Colev	695
Coli	696
Coll	697
Collet	698
Colli	699
Collin	699
Colling	711
Collingwood	711
Collins	712
Collins, S.	713
Collo	714
Colly	715
Colm	716
Coln	717
Colo	718

Colon	719	Conc	744	Cool	774
Colp	721	Cond	745	Coom	775
Colq	722	Condo	746	Coomaraswamy	775
Cols	723	Cone	747	Coop	776
Colt	724	Conf	748	Cooper	777
Colto	725	Conference	748	Cooper, H.	777
Colu	726	Cong	749	Cooper, O.	778
Colv	727	Congress	749	Coot	779
Coly	727	Coni	751	Cop	781
Com	728	Conk	752	Cope	782
Comar	728	Cono	753	Copi	783
Comaromi	728	Conr	754	Copl	784
Comb	729	Cons	755	Copp	785
Combes	731	Const	756	Copr	785
Come	732	Constan	757	Coq	786
Comi	733	Constanti	758	Cor	787
Comm	734	Consul	758	Coran	788
Command	734	Cont	759	Corb	789
Commission	734	Conte	761	Corbett	789
Committee	734	Conti	762	Corbin	791
Communist	734	Conto	763	Corbo	792
Como	735	Contr	764	Corc	793
Comp	736	Contu	765	Cord	794
Compan	737	Conv	766	Cordi	795
Complan	737	Conw	767	Cordo	796
Compt	738	Cony	768	Core	797
Computer	738	Conze	768	Corelli	797
Coms	739	Coo	769	Cori	798
Comt	741	Cook	771	Cork	799
Comy	742	Cooke	772	Corl	799
Con	743	Cooke, M.	773	Corm	811

Corn	812
Corne	813
Cornel	814
Corner	815
Cornet	816
Cornh	817
Corni	818
Corno	819
Cornw	821
Coro	822
Corp	789
Corr	823
Corre	824
Corri	825
Corrlia	824
Cors	826
Cort	827
Cortes	828
Corti	829
Corto	831
Corv	832
Cory	833
Cos	834
Cosp	835
Coss	836
Cost	837
Costan	838
Coste	839
Costel	841
Coster	842
Cot	843
Coti	844
Coto	845
Cott	846
Cotter	847
Cotti	848
Cottl	849
Cotto	851
Cotton	851
Coty	852
Cou	853
Coud	854
Coul	855
Coulter	855
Coum	856
Council	855
Coup	857
Coupl	857
Cour	858
Courc	859
Courl	861
Court	862
Courte	863
Courti	864
Courtn	865
Courto	866
Cous	867
Couss	868
Coust	869
Cout	871
Coutu	872
Cov	873
Covid	873
Cow	874
Cowasjee	874
Cowell	874
Cowl	875
Cowp	876
Cox	877
Cox, R.	878
Coxe	879
Coy	881
Coz	882
Cr	883
Crae	884
Craf	885
Crai	886
Craik	887
Crak	888
Cram	889
Cran	891
Cranefield	891
Crao	892
Crap	893
Cras	894
Crat	895
Crato	896
Crau	897
Crav	898
Craven	898
Craw	899
Crawford	899
Crawl	911

Cre	912	Crom	945	Cunn	973
Cree	913	Cromw	946	Cunnigham	973
Crei	914	Cron	947	Cup	974
Crel	915	Croo	948	Cur	975
Creo	916	Crook	948	Curie	975
Crep	917	Cros	949	Curr	976
Creq	918	Crosby	949	Currimbhoy	976
Cres	919	Cross	949	Curs	977
Cresp	921	Crou	952	Curt	978
Cress	922	Crough	952	Curtis, J.	979
Cresw	923	Crow	953	Curtis, P.	981
Cret	924	Croy	954	Curw	982
Creto	924	Cru	955	Curx	983
Creu	925	Crum	956	Curz	983
Crev	926	Crus	957	Curzen	983
Crew	927	Crystal	957	Cus	984
Cri	928	Cs	958	Cushing, M.	985
Cril	929	Ct	959	Cushm	986
Crin	931	Cu	961	Cust	987
Cris	932	Cub	962	Cut	988
Crist	933	Cuc	963	Cutl	989
Crit	934	Cud	964	Cutler	989
Critt	935	Cue	965	Cutt	991
Criv	936	Cui	966	Cutter	991
Cro	937	Cul	967	Cuv	992
Crock	938	Culp	968	Cuy	993
Croe	939	Cum	969	Cy	994
Crof	941	Cumm	971	Cyc	995
Croi	942	Cumminingham	971	Cyl	996
Crok	943	Cummins	971	Cyr	997
Crol	944	Cun	972	Cz	998

Czo	999

D

D'Souza	111
Da costa	111
Da	111
Dabas	111
Dabholkar	111
Dabi	112
Dabl	113
Dabn	114
Dabo	115
Dabr	116
Dabur	116
Dac	117
Daci	118
Dacr	119
Dad	121
Dada	121
Dae	122
Dael	123
Daf	124
Dag	125
Dagar	125
Dagi	126
Dagli	126
Dago	127
Dagu	128
Dah	129
Dahiwala	129
Dahiya	129
Dahl	131
Dahlberg	131
Dai	132
Dail	133
Daily	133
Dair	134
Daisy	134
Dak	135
Dal	136
Dalai	136
Dalal	136
Dalb	137
Dalbir	137
Dalc	138
Dale	139
Dales	141
Dalg	142
Dalh	143
Dalip	143
Daljeet	143
Dall	144
Dallas	145
Dalle	146
Dalli	147
Dalm	148
Dalp	149
Dalr	151
Dalrymple	151
Dalt	152
Dalton	152
Dalvi	152
Daly	153
Dam	154
Daman	154
Damas	155
Damb	156
Dame	157
Dami	158
Damin	159
Damis	161
Damle	161
Damm	162
Damo	163
Damodar	163
Damop	164
Damp	165
Dampi	166
Dan	167
Dana	168
Dana, H.	168
Dana, M.	169
Dana, S.	171
Danb	172
Danc	173
Dancer	173
Danck	174
Danco	175
Dand	176
Danda	176
Dandapani	176
Dandekar	176
Dando	177
Dandr	178

Dandvate	178
Dane	179
Danf	181
Dang	182
Dange	182
Dangwal	182
Dani	183
Daniel	184
Daniell	185
Daniels	186
Danish	186
Dank	187
Dann	188
Danp	189
Dans	191
Dant	192
Danti	193
Danto	194
Dantwala	194
Dantz	195
Danv	196
Danvi	197
Dany	198
Danz	199
Dao	211
Dap	212
Dar	213
Darbar	213
Darc	214
Dard	215
Darde	216
Dare	217
Dari	218
Dark	219
Darl	221
Darling	221
Darm	222
Darn	223
Daro	224
Daroga	224
Darr	225
Darshan	225
Dart	226
Daru	227
Daruwala	227
Darw	228
Das	229
Dasear	229
Dasgupta	229
Dass	231
Dastur	231
Daswani	231
Dat	232
Data	232
Datar	232
Date	232
Dath	233
Dati	234
Datt	234
Datta	234
Dau	235
Daubi	236
Dauc	237
Daud	238
Daud	238
Daul	239
Daulat	239
Daum	241
Daun	242
Daur	243
Daus	244
Dav	245
Dave	246
Davent	247
Daver	248
Daves	248
Davi	249
Davics	249
David	249
Davids	251
Davidson	252
Davidson, M.	253
Davie	254
Davies	255
Davies, J.	256
Davies, T	257
Davig	258
Davil	259
Davis	261
Davis, H.	262
Davis, M.	263
Davis, S.	264
Davis, W.	265

Davo	266	Dec	291	Dekr	329
Davos	266	Decap	291	Del	331
Davr	267	Dece	292	Del	331
Davy	268	Dech	293	Delac	332
Daw	269	Deci	294	Delaf	333
Dawk	271	Deck	295	Delai	334
Daws	272	Deco	296	Delal	335
Dawson	272	Decour	297	Delam	336
Day	273	Decr	298	Delan	337
Day, J.	274	Ded	299	Delap	338
Day, S.	275	Dee	311	Delar	339
Daya	275	Deegan	311	Delat	341
Dayal	275	Deep	311	Delau	342
Dayanand	275	Deepak	311	Delav	343
Dayt	276	Deer	312	Delb	344
Daz	277	Def	313	Delc	345
De silva	278	Defo	314	Dele	346
De souza	278	Defor	315	Deles	347
De	278	Defr	316	Deleu	348
Deal	279	Deg	317	Delf	349
Dean	281	Degl	318	Delfo	351
Dean, M.	282	Dego	319	Delg	352
Dean,K	281	Degr	321	Delhi	352
Deane	283	Deh	322	Deli	353
Deane, M.	284	Deho	323	Delis	354
Dear	285	Dei	324	Deliu	355
Deb	286	Deis	325	Delk	356
Debo	287	Dej	326	Dell	357
Debr	288	Dejo	327	Dello	358
Debroy	288	Dek	328	Delm	359
Debu	289	Deka	328	Delo	361

Delor	362
Delp	363
Delr	364
Dels	365
Delt	366
Delv	367
Delz	368
Dem	369
Deman	371
Demar	372
Demas	373
Demb	374
Dembo	375
Deme	376
Demet	377
Demi	378
Demid	379
Demil	381
Demm	382
Demo	383
Demon	384
Demop	385
Demor	386
Demos	387
Demou	388
Demp	389
Den	391
Dene	392
Deng	392
Denh	393
Deni	394
Denis	395
Denison	396
Denm	397
Denn	398
Denner	399
Denni	411
Denning	411
Denny	412
Deno	413
Dent	414
Denton	415
Denv	416
Deny	417
Deo	418
Deodhar	418
Deogaonkar	418
Deol	418
Deora	418
Dep	419
Department	419
Depl	421
Depo	422
Depp	423
Depr	424
Depu	425
Deq	426
Der	427
Derby, M.	428
Derc	429
Dere	431
Derh	432
Deri	433
Derl	434
Derm	435
Dern	436
Dero	437
Derr	438
Derret	438
Derw	439
Des	441
Desai	441
Desau	442
Desb	443
Desbo	444
Desc	445
Desch	446
Descl	447
Desco	448
Descr	449
Dese	451
Deses	452
Desf	453
Desg	454
Desgr	455
Desh	456
Deshbandhu	456
Deshmukh	456
Deshpande	456
Deshta	456
Desi	457
Desikachar	457
Desit	458

Desj	459
Desl	461
Deslo	462
Desm	463
Desmo	464
Desmou	465
Desn	466
Deso	467
Desp	468
Despl	469
Despo	471
Despor	472
Despr	473
Desr	474
Dess	475
Dest	476
Destr	477
Desv	478
Deswal	478
Det	479
Deti	481
Deto	482
Detr	483
Detz	484
Deu	485
Deus	486
Deutch	486
Deux	487
Dev	488
Deva	488
Deve	489
Dever	491
Devg	491
Devi	492
Devig	493
Devil	494
Devin	495
Devinder	495
Devis	496
Devl	497
Devo	498
Devon	499
Devons	511
Devos	512
Devot	513
Devr	514
Dew	515
Dewan	515
Dewe	516
Dewes	517
Dewet	518
Dewett	518
Dewey	519
Dewi	521
Dewitt	522
Dewitt, M.	523
Dewl	524
Dex	525
Dext	526
Dexter, M.	527
Dey	528
Deyn	529
Deys	531
Dez	532
Dh	533
Dhakad	533
Dhaky	533
Dhal	533
Dhaliwal	533
Dhall	533
Dhameja	533
Dhami	533
Dhanpat	533
Dhar	533
Dharam	533
Dhavalikar	533
Dhawan	533
Dhe	534
Dheer	534
Dhenkey	534
Dhesi	534
Dhillon	534
Dhiman	534
Dhinds	534
Dhir	534
Dho	535
Dhody	535
Dholakia	535
Dhoni	535
Dhoot	535
Dhown	535
Dhumal	535
Dhurva	535

Dhyane	535	Diel	561	Ding	584
Di	536	Dien	562	Dini	585
Diak	536	Dier	563	Dinkar	585
Diam	537	Dies	564	Dino	586
Diamond	537	Diet	565	Dins	587
Dian	538	Dietr	566	Dio	588
Diana	538	Dieu	567	Diod	589
Diap	539	Diez	568	Diog	591
Dias	541	Dif	569	Dion	592
Diaz	542	Dig	571	Diop	593
Dib	543	Dige	572	Dios	594
Dibd	544	Digg	573	Diot	595
Dibrugarh	544	Digh	574	Dip	596
Dic	545	Dighe	574	Dir	597
Dice	546	Dign	575	Dirc	598
Dicey	546	Digvijya	575	Directory	598
Dichonary	554	Dikshit	575	Dirk	599
Dick	547	Dikshitar	575	Dis	611
Dicke	548	Dil	576	Discrict	614
Dicker	549	Dilawar	576	Disn	612
Dickey	551	Dilbagh	576	Disr	613
Dicki	552	Dilip	576	Dissanayak	613
Dickinso	553	Dilk	577	Dist	614
Dickinson	553	Dill	578	District	614
Dicks	554	Dillo	579	Dit	615
Dictionary	554	Dilw	581	Dits	616
Did	555	Dilwali	581	Ditt	617
Didi	556	Dim	582	Div	618
Dido	557	Din	583	Divakar	618
Didr	558	Dindayal	583	Divec	618
Die	559	Dinesh	583	Divedi	618

Divekar	618	Dodds	642	Domit	672
Divya	618	Dode	643	Domn	673
Diwakar	618	Dodg	644	Don	674
Diwan	618	Dodge, M.	645	Dona	674
Dix	619	Dodi	646	Donal	675
Dixit	619	Dodiya	646	Donald	675
Dixo	621	Dods	647	Donalds	676
Dixon	621	Dods	647	Donat	677
Dixw	622	Dodwell	648	Donc	678
Dj	623	Doe	649	Dond	679
Dje	624	Doel	651	Done	681
Dji	625	Doer	652	Dong	682
Djo	626	Does	653	Dongre	682
Dm	627	Dog	654	Doni	683
Dmi	628	Dogra	654	Donk	684
Dmo	629	Doh	655	Donn	685
Do	631	Dohn	656	Donnald	685
Doaba	631	Doi	657	Donner	686
Doabia	631	Dois	658	Dono	687
Dob	632	Dol	659	Donz	689
Dobb	632	Dolb	661	Doo	691
Dobe	633	Dolc	662	Dool	691
Dobr	634	Dole	663	Doolnbos	691
Dobs	635	Dolg	664	Dop	692
Doc	636	Doll	665	Dor	693
Doch	637	Dom	666	Doraiswami	693
Doctor	637	Domb	667	Dorat	694
Document	637	Dome	668	Dorc	695
Dod	638	Domi	669	Dore	695
Dodd	639	Domin	671	Dori	696
Doddr	641	Dominic	671	Dorig	697

Dorio	698	Douglas, W.	737	Drake, S.	763
Doris	699	Doul	738	Dran	764
Dorji	699	Dour	739	Drap	765
Dorl	711	Dous	741	Draper, M.	766
Dorm	712	Douv	742	Drapp	767
Dorn	713	Dov	743	Drapper	767
Dorni	714	Doval	743	Dravid	767
Doro	715	Dove	743	Dray	768
Dorr	716	Dow	744	Drayt	769
Dors	717	Dowd	745	Dre	771
Dorse	718	Dowdy	745	Drel	772
Dort	719	Dowe	746	Dres	773
Dorv	721	Dowl	747	Dreu	774
Dos	722	Down	748	Drev	775
Dosajh	722	Downe	748	Drew	776
Doshi	722	Downh	749	Drex	777
Dosi	723	Downi	751	Drey	778
Doss	724	Dows	752	Dreze	778
Dost	724	Dowsar	752	Dri	779
Dot	725	Doy	753	Drink	781
Dou	726	Doyl	754	Driv	782
Doubl	727	Doyle	754	Dro	783
Douc	728	Doz	755	Drog	784
Doue	729	Dr	756	Drol	785
Doug	731	Drab	756	Drom	786
Dough	732	Drac	757	Dron	786
Dougl	733	Drae	758	Dros	787
Douglas	734	Drag	759	Drou	788
Douglas, G.	734	Drak	761	Drouno	789
Douglas, M.	735	Drake	762	Drov	791
Douglas, S.	736	Drake, M.	762	Droy	792

Droz	793	Duch	826	Duffy	858
Dru	794	Duchat	827	Dufl	859
Drucker	794	Duche	828	Dufo	861
Drum	795	Duches	829	Dufourn	862
Drur	796	Duchi	831	Dufr	863
Drury	796	Ducho	832	Dufres	864
Drus	797	Duci	833	Dufu	865
Dry	798	Duck	834	Dug	866
Dryd	799	Ducke	835	Dugal	866
Dryden	799	Duckw	836	Duggal	866
Drys	811	Ducl	837	Dugo	867
Dsw	622	Duclo	838	Dugu	868
Du	812	Duco	839	Duh	869
Dua	812	Ducon	841	Duhe	871
Duarah	812	Ducr	842	Duho	872
Dub	813	Ducro	843	Dui	873
Dubai	813	Dud	844	Duil	874
Dubashi	813	Dude	845	Duis	875
Dube	814	Dudeja	845	Duj	876
Dubey	814	Dudi	846	Duk	877
Dubin	814	Dudl	847	Dul	878
Dubo	815	Dudley, L.	848	Dulat	878
Dubois, M.	816	Dudley, S.	849	Dulau	879
Dubos	817	Dudo	851	Dulc	881
Dubou	818	Due	852	Duli	882
Dubr	819	Duer	853	Dull	883
Dubu	821	Duf	854	Dulo	884
Duc	822	Duff	855	Dum	885
Ducar	823	Duffe	856	Dumas	886
Ducas	824	Duffi	857	Dumay	887
Duce	825	Duffrin	857	Dume	888

Dumm	889	Dupe	932	Duriv	963
Dumo	891	Duperr	933	Duro	964
Dumon	892	Dupi	934	Durr	965
Dumont	893	Dupl	935	Durrane	965
Dumor	894	Duples	936	Durs	966
Dumou	895	Dupo	937	Duru	967
Dumour	896	Dupont	938	Duruy	968
Dun	897	Dupor	939	Dury	969
Dunb	898	Dupp	941	Dus	971
Dunbar	899	Dupr	942	Duse	972
Dunc	911	Dupres	943	Dusi	973
Duncan	912	Dupu	944	Duss	974
Duncan, M.	912	Dupuy	945	Dut	975
Dunco	913	Duq	946	Dutch	975
Dund	914	Dur	947	Duti	976
Dundo	915	Duran	948	Duto	977
Dung	916	Durand, M.	949	Dutr	978
Dunh	917	Durant	951	Dutt	979
Duni	918	Duras	952	Dutta	979
Dunk	919	Duraz	953	Dutton	981
Dunl	921	Durd	954	Duv	982
Dunlo	922	Dure	955	Duval	983
Dunlop	922	Duret	956	Duvau	984
Dunn	923	Durey	957	Duve	985
Dunni	924	Durf	958	Duvet	986
Duno	925	Durfo	959	Duvi	987
Duns	926	Durga	959	Duy	988
Dunt	927	Durgeoh	959	Dw	989
Dunu	928	Durgh	959	Dwarka	989
Dup	929	Durh	961	Dwi	991
Dupar	931	Duri	962	Dwight, J.	992

Dwight, S.	993
Dwivedi	993
Dy	994
Dyal	994
Dye	995
Dyer	996
Dym	997
Dyr	998
Dyson	998
Dz	999

E

Ea	11
Eagle	11
Eakin	11
Eam	12
Eas	13
East	14
Eastesn	14
Eat	14
Eaton	14
Eazekiel	14
Eb	15
Eber	16
Ec	17
Ech	18
Eck	19
Economic	19
Ed	21
Edef	22
Edg	23
Edger	23
Edit	23
Edleman	23
Edm	24
Education	24
Edw	25
Edward	26
Edwards	26
Ef	27
Eg	28
Ege	29
Egg	29
Egl	31
Egr	32
Eh	33
Ei	34
Eid	34
Ein	35
Einsteen	35
Einstein	35
Eis	36
Eisen	36
Ejaz	36
Ekbote	36
El	37
Elder	37
Elea	38
Elen	39
Elg	41
Eli	42
Elior	42
Elis	43
Elizabelh	43
Ell	44
Elle	45
Elli	46
Ellior	46
Ellis	47
Elm	48
Elora	48
Els	49
Elt	51
Elw	52
Em	53
Emerson	53
Emkar	53
Emm	54
Emp	55
En	56
Enayat	56
Encyclopedia	56
Eng	57
Engineer	57
Engl	58
English	58
Enn	59
Ent	61
Eo	62
Ep	63
Epi	64
Er	65
Erd	66
Ere	67

Eri	68
Erin	68
Erl	69
Erm	71
Err	72
Ers	73
Es	74
Esd	75
Esl	76
Esp	77
Esperanza	77
Ess	78
Essay	78
Est	79
Esteves	79
Esti	81
Estr	82
Eswara	82
Et	83
Eth	84
Etienne	84
Eto	85
Eu	86
Eug	87
Eugene	87
Eul	88
Eup	89
Euro	89
Europe	89
Eus	91
Ev	92
Evans	92
Eve	93
Ever	93
Ew	94
Ewb	94
Ewi	95
Ex	96
Exim	96
Ey	97
Eyr	98
Ez	99

F

Fa	111
Fab	112
Fabb	113
Fabe	114
Faber	115
Faberi	116
Fabert	117
Fabi	118
Fabil	119
Fabiu	121
Fabr	122
Fabre	123
Fabri	124
Fabrian	125
Fabric	126
Fabrin	127
Fabris	128
Fabriz	129
Fabro	131
Fabrot	132
Fabry	133
Fabu	134
Fabv	135
Faby	136
Fac	137
Faccio	138
Fach	139
Faci	141
Facis	142
Facu	143
Fad	144
Fadi	145
Fadl	146
Fae	147
Faen	148
Faes	149
Fag	151
Fage	152
Fagel	153
Fagg	154
Fagi	155
Fagn	156
Fah	157
Fahr	158
Fai	159
Fail	161
Fain	162
Fair	163
Fairban	164
Fairc	165

Fairf	166	Fallet	195	Farley, M.	232
Fairfax, M.	167	Fallo	196	Farm	233
Fairfie	168	Fallow	196	Farmer	234
Fairfield, M.	169	Fals	197	Farmer, M.	234
Fairh	171	Fam	198	Farn	235
Fairl	172	Family	198	Farnh	236
Fais	173	Fan	199	Faro	237
Faisal	174	Fane	211	Farooq	237
Fait	174	Fani	212	Faroori	237
Faiv	175	Fann	213	Farq	238
Faiz	175	Fano	214	Farr	239
Faizi	175	Fans	215	Farran	241
Fak	176	Fant	216	Farrar	242
Fakir	176	Fanto	217	Farrar, J.	243
Fal	177	Fantu	218	Farrar, S.	244
Falc	178	Fap	218	Farre	245
Falck	179	Faq	218	Farrell	245
Falco	181	Far	219	Farri	246
Falcone	182	Fara	219	Fars	247
Falconer, M.	183	Farc	221	Farurui	247
Falconet	184	Fare	222	Fas	248
Falcu	185	Farg	223	Fass	249
Fald	186	Fari	224	Fast	251
Falder	186	Farid	224	Fat	252
Fale	187	Faridi	224	Fateh	252
Falg	188	Farin	225	Father	252
Fali	189	Faring	226	Fati	253
Falk	191	Farini	227	Fato	254
Falken	192	Faris	228	Fau	255
Falkn	193	Farj	229	Fauch	256
Fall	194	Farl	231	Fauci	257

Faud	258	Fe	288	Felv	329
Faug	259	Feb	289	Fen	331
Fauja	259	Fec	291	Fene	332
Faul	261	Fed	292	Feni	333
Faulh	262	Feder	293	Fenn	334
Faulk	263	Fedirahm	293	Fennel	335
Faun	264	Fedo	294	Fenner	336
Faur	265	Fee	295	Fenni	337
Fauri	266	Feh	296	Fenno	338
Faus	267	Fei	297	Feno	339
Fausti	268	Feildi	298	Fens	341
Fausto	268	Fein	299	Fent	342
Faustu	269	Feit	311	Fenw	343
Fauv	271	Fel	311	Feo	344
Fav	272	Feld	312	Fer	345
Fave	273	Feldman	312	Ferb	346
Favi	274	Feli	313	Ferd	347
Favo	275	Felic	314	Ferdo	348
Favr	276	Felin	315	Fere	349
Favre	277	Felix	316	Ferg	351
Faw	278	Fell	317	Fergu	352
Fawcetf	278	Felle	318	Ferguson	353
Fawe	279	Felli	319	Ferguson, M.	353
Fawk	281	Fello	321	Ferguss	354
Fay	282	Fellow	322	Ferh	355
Faye	283	Felo	323	Feri	356
Fayet	284	Fels	324	Ferl	357
Fayo	285	Felt	325	Ferm	358
Fayt	286	Felto	326	Ferme	359
Faz	287	Felton, M.	327	Fermi	358
Fazal	287	Feltr	328	Fermo	361

Fern	362	Ferris	394	Ffa	436
Fernades	362	Ferro	395	Ffo	437
Fernand	363	Ferron	396	Fi	438
Ferne	364	Ferrou	397	Fiam	439
Ferni	365	Ferru	398	Fian	441
Ferno	366	Ferry	399	Fias	442
Fero	367	Fert	411	Fib	443
Ferr	368	Feru	412	Fic	444
Ferradane	368	Fes	413	Fich	445
Ferral	369	Fessen	414	Fici	446
Ferram	371	Fessenden, M.	415	Fick	447
Ferran	372	Fessi	416	Fico	448
Ferrant	373	Fessl	417	Fid	449
Ferrar	374	Fest	418	Fide	451
Ferrari	375	Festival	418	Fie	452
Ferraro	376	Fet	419	Field	453
Ferrars	377	Fett	421	Field, H.	454
Ferrary	378	Feu	422	Field, M.	455
Ferrat	379	Feuer	423	Field, S.	456
Ferrau	381	Feug	424	Field, W.	457
Ferre	382	Feui	425	Fielde	458
Ferrei	383	Feuill	426	Fieldi	459
Ferreo	384	Feut	427	Fields	461
Ferrer	385	Fev	428	Fields, J.	462
Ferrero	386	Fevr	429	Fields, S.	463
Ferret	387	Fevret	431	Fien	464
Ferri	388	Few	432	Fier	465
Ferrib	389	Fey	433	Fies	466
Ferrie	391	Feyer	434	Fiesco	467
Ferrin	392	Feyn	435	Fieso	468
Ferrio	393	Feynman	435	Fif	469

Fig	471
Figi	472
Figo	473
Figr	474
Figu	475
Figui	476
Figul	477
Fil	478
Filas	479
File	481
Fili	482
Filip	483
Fill	484
Fille	485
Filli	486
Fillizor	486
Film	487
Filo	488
Fils	489
Fin	491
Finch	492
Finck	493
Find	494
Fine	495
Finet	496
Fing	497
Fini	498
Fink	499
Finl	511
Finland	511
Finlays	512
Finley	513
Finn	514
Fino	515
Fins	516
Fio	517
Fiore	518
Fiori	519
Fiorin	521
Fir	522
Fire	523
Firm	524
Firmin	525
Firn	526
Firo	527
Fis	528
Fische	529
Fischer	529
Fise	531
Fish	532
Fisher	533
Fisher, J.	534
Fisher, M.	535
Fisher, S.	536
Fisher, W.	537
Fisk	538
Fisk, M.	539
Fiske	541
Fiske, M.	542
Fiss	543
Fit	544
Fitch, J.	545
Fitch, S.	546
Fitt	547
Fitz	548
Fitza	549
Fitzb	551
Fitzc	552
Fitzg	553
Fitzgerald, M.	554
Fitzh	555
Fitzj	556
Fitzm	557
Fitzn	558
Fitzp	559
Fitzr	561
Fitzs	562
Fitzt	563
Fitzw	564
Fiu	565
Fix	566
Fiz	567
Fl	568
Flac	569
Flach	571
Flaco	572
Flad	573
Flag	574
Flah	575
Flai	576
Flam	577
Flamen	578
Flami	579

Flamm	581	Flin	622	Fog	655
Flams	582	Flint	623	Fogl	656
Flan	583	Flint, J.	624	Foh	657
Fland	584	Flint, S.	625	Foi	658
Flandr	585	Flip	626	Foin	659
Flat	586	Flit	627	Foix	661
Flau	587	Flo	628	Fok	662
Flav	588	Flog	629	Fol	663
Flavi	589	Floo	631	Folg	664
Flavu	591	Flor	632	Foli	665
Flax	592	Florent	633	Folk	666
Fle	593	Flores	634	Foll	667
Flee	594	Flori	635	Folli	668
Fleet	594	Florid	636	Folq	669
Fleetw	595	Florin	637	Fols	671
Flei	596	Florio	638	Fom	672
Fleig	596	Floris	639	Fon	673
Flem	597	Floru	641	Fonf	674
Fleming, M.	598	Flot	642	Fonn	675
Flemm	599	Flott	643	Fons	676
Fles	611	Flow	644	Fonseca	676
Flet	612	Floy	645	Fonseea	676
Fletcher	613	Floyd	645	Font	677
Fletcher, J.	613	Flu	646	Fontai	678
Fletcher, P.	614	Flur	647	Fontan	679
Fletcher, S.	615	Fly	648	Fontani	681
Fleu	616	Fo	649	Fonte	682
Fleuri	617	Fob	651	Fonten	683
Fleury	618	Foc	652	Fonti	684
Flex	619	Fod	653	Fontr	685
Fli	621	Foe	654	Foo	686

Food	686	Formo	726	Foster, S.	757
Foot	687	Forn	727	Foster, W.	758
Foote	688	Forr	728	Fot	759
Foote, M.	689	Forrest, M.	729	Fother	761
Fop	691	Forrester	731	Fou	762
For	692	Fors	732	Fouch	763
Forbes	693	Forst	733	Foud	764
Forbes, H.	693	Forster	734	Foug	765
Forbes, M.	694	Forster, M.	734	Foui	766
Forbes, S.	695	Forsy	735	Foul	767
Forbi	696	Fort	736	Foulo	768
Forc	697	Forte	737	Foulq	769
Forch	698	Fortes	738	Foun	771
Ford	699	Forth	739	Found	771
Ford, M.	711	Forti	741	Foundrlin	771
Fordh	712	Fortin	742	Fouq	772
Fordy	713	Fortis	743	Four	773
Fore	714	Forto	744	Fourer	774
Foreem	714	Fortu	745	Fouri	775
Foreign	714	Fortune	745	Fourm	776
Forem	715	Fos	746	Fourn	777
Fores	716	Fosc	747	Fourni	778
Forest	716	Fosd	748	Fourniv	779
Forester	717	Fosg	749	Fourq	781
Foresti	718	Foskett	749	Fout	782
Forf	719	Foss	751	Fov	783
Forg	721	Fosse	752	Fow	784
Forl	722	Fost	753	Fowl	785
Form	723	Foster	754	Fowler	786
Forman	724	Foster, H.	755	Fowler, H.	786
Forme	725	Foster, M.	756	Fowler, M.	787

Fowler, S.	788	Franklin, H.	832	Freh	861
Fowler, W.	789	Franklin, M.	833	Frei	862
Fox	791	Franklin, S.	834	Freig	863
Fox, H.	792	Franq	835	Freil	864
Fox, M.	793	Frant	836	Freim	865
Fox, S.	794	Franz	837	Freir	866
Foxe	795	Frap	838	Frek	867
Foy	796	Frar	839	Frel	868
Fr	797	Fras	841	Frem	869
Frach	798	Fraser	842	Fremi	871
Frad	799	Fraser, M.	842	Fremo	872
Frag	811	Frass	843	Fren	873
Frai	812	Frat	844	French	874
Fram	813	Frau	845	French, H.	874
Framji	813	Frauwall	845	French, M.	875
Fran	814	Frav	846	French, S.	876
France	815	Frawley	846	French, W.	877
Franch	816	Fray	847	Frend	878
Franci	817	Fraz	848	Freni	879
Francis	818	Fre	849	Frer	881
Francis, M.	819	Frec	851	Freret	882
Franciu	821	Fred	852	Frero	883
Franck	822	Fredrick	852	Fres	884
Francke	823	Free	853	Fresh	885
Franckl	824	Freel	854	Fresn	886
Franco	825	Freem	855	Fress	887
Francon	826	Freeman	855	Fret	888
Frang	827	Freer	856	Freu	889
Frank	828	Frees	857	Frev	891
Franke	829	Freg	858	Frew	892
Frankl	831	Frego	859	Frey	893

Freyl	894
Freyt	895
Frez	896
Fri	897
Frid	898
Frie	899
Friedl	911
Fries	912
Fril	913
Frin	914
Frip	915
Frir	916
Fris	917
Frisw	918
Frit	919
Friz	921
Fro	922
Frobi	923
Froc	924
Froe	925
Froel	926
Frog	927
Froh	928
Froi	929
From	931
Fromm	932
Fron	933
Frons	934
Front	935
Fronto	936
Fror	937
Fros	938
Frost	939
Frot	941
Frou	942
Frow	943
Fru	944
Frun	945
Fry	946
Fry, M.	947
Frye	948
Fu	949
Fuchs	951
Fud	952
Fue	953
Fuen	954
Fues	955
Fuf	956
Fug	957
Fugg	958
Fuh	959
Fui	961
Ful	962
Fulg	963
Fulk	964
Full	965
Fuller	966
Fuller, H.	966
Fuller, M.	967
Fuller, S.	968
Fuller, W.	969
Fullert	971
Fullo	972
Fulm	973
Fult	974
Fulv	975
Fum	976
Fume	977
Fumi	978
Fun	979
Fund	981
Funk	982
Funn	983
Fur	983
Furer	983
Furi	984
Furl	985
Furm	986
Furn	987
Furnes	988
Furni	989
Furs	991
Furt	992
Fus	993
Fuss	994
Fust	995
Fusu	996
Futehally	996
Fy	997
Fyo	998
Fyr	999
Fyzee	999

G

Ga	111
Gab	112
Gabbar	116
Gabi	113
Gabio	114
Gabl	115
Gabo	116
Gabor	116
Gabr	117
Gabriel	118
Gabro	119
Gac	121
Gaco	122
Gad	123
Gade	124
Gadgill	124
Gadhi	124
Gadhok	124
Gadkar	124
Gado	125
Gadre	125
Gads	126
Gae	127
Gaer	128
Gaeret	128
Gaet	129
Gaf	131
Gag	132
Gagan	132
Gage, M.	133
Gagi	134
Gagl	135
Gago	136
Gahlor	136
Gahlot	136
Gahos	427
Gai	137
Gai	137
Gaikwad	137
Gail	138
Gaill	139
Gaim	141
Gain	142
Gaind	142
Gains	143
Gair	144
Gairola	144
Gaj	145
Gajanan	145
Gajendrajadkar	145
Gajja	145
Gajrani	145
Gajwani	145
Gakhar	145
Gal	146
Galander	146
Galau	147
Galb	148
Galbraith	148
Gald	149
Gale	151
Gale, M.	152
Galen	153
Galer	154
Galf	155
Gali	156
Galig	157
Galil	158
Galit	159
Galitz	161
Gall	162
Gallan	163
Gallat	164
Gallau	165
Galle	166
Gallet	167
Galli	168
Gallim	169
Gallio	171
Gallo	172
Gallois	173
Gallow	174
Gallu	175
Gallus	176
Gallw	177
Galo	178
Galt	179
Galto	181
Galv	182
Galw	183
Gam	184
Gamai	185

Gamal	186	Ganpati	198	Garl	233
Gamb	187	Gans	199	Garn	234
Gambar	188	Gant	211	Garner	234
Gambe	189	Gant	211	Garnet	235
Gambhir	189	Gantzer	211	Garni	236
Gambi	191	Gaonkar	211	Garo	236
Gambia	191	Gar	212	Garog	237
Gamble	191	Garb	213	Garr	238
Gambo	192	Garbo	214	Garre	239
Gamm	193	Garc	215	Garri	241
Gamo	194	Garci	216	Garris	242
Gan	195	Gard	217	Garro	243
Ganda	195	Gard	219	Gart	244
Gandhi	195	Garde	218	Garz	245
Gandhigram	195	Gardi	219	Gas	246
Gando	196	Gardiner	221	Gasco	247
Gandotra	196	Gardiner, H.	222	Gask	248
Ganesan	196	Gardiner, M.	223	Gaskell	248
Ganesh	196	Gardiner, S.	224	Gasp	249
Ganesopadhyay	196	Gardn	225	Gass	251
Gang	197	Gardner	226	Gassel	251
Ganga	197	Gardner	226	Gasset	252
Gangal	197	Gardner, H.	227	Gassi	253
Gangdhara	197	Gardner, P.	228	Gasso	254
Gangnly	197	Gare	229	Gast	255
Gangopadhya	197	Gareha	229	Gaston	256
Gangrade	197	Gareia	229	Gastr	257
Gangwel	197	Garf	231	Gat	258
Ganjoo	197	Garg	231	Gates	259
Ganju	197	Garhwre	231	Gati	261
Gann	198	Gari	232	Gatt	262

Gatti	263
Gau	264
Gauba	264
Gauc	265
Gaud	266
Gaudi	267
Gauf	268
Gauhar	268
Gaul	269
Gault	271
Gaun	272
Gaur	273
Gauri	273
Gaus	274
Gaut	275
Gautam	275
Gauth	276
Gauti	277
Gauz	278
Gav	279
Gavai	279
Gavaskar	279
Gavau	281
Gave	282
Gavi	283
Gavin	283
Gaw	284
Gay	285
Gaye	286
Gaykaved	286
Gayl	287
Gayo	288
Gaytri	288
Gaz	289
Gazetteer	289
Gazo	291
Ge	292
Geb	293
Gec	294
Ged	295
Gedam	295
Gedl	296
Gee	297
Geelani	297
Geer	298
Geeta	298
Gef	299
Geh	311
Gehlawat	311
Gehlot	311
Gei	312
Geis	313
Gel	314
Geld	315
Gele	316
Geli	317
Gell	318
Gelli	319
Gelo	321
Gem	322
Gemini	322
Gemm	323
Gen	324
Gend	325
Gene	326
Genelia	326
General	326
Genes	327
Genet	328
Geng	329
Geni	331
Genl	332
Genn	333
Genne	334
Geno	335
Gens	336
Gent	337
Gentil	338
Gentr	339
Genu	341
Geo	342
Geof	343
Geoffery	343
Geoffri	344
Geoffro	345
Geograp	345
Geological	345
Geor	346
George	347
George, G.	348
George, H	349
Georges	351
Georgi	352

Gep	353
Ger	354
Geran	355
Gerar	356
Gerard, M.	357
Gerardi	358
Gerau	359
Gerb	361
Gerber	362
Gerbi	363
Gerbo	364
Gerc	365
Gerd	366
Gere	367
Gerh	368
Geri	369
Gerl	371
Germ	372
German	373
Germi	374
Germo	375
Gern	376
Gero	377
Gerr	378
Gerry	379
Gers	381
Gerso	382
Gerst	383
Gert	384
Gerv	385
Gervas	386
Gervi	387
Gery	388
Ges	389
Gesmam	389
Gesn	391
Gess	392
Gest	393
Get	394
Getty	394
Geu	395
Gev	396
Gey	397
Gez	398
Gfi	399
Gh	411
Ghai	411
Ghaiye	411
Ghali	411
Ghalib	411
Ghan	411
Ghatage	411
Ghatak	411
Ghei	412
Gher	413
Gherard	414
Gherardi	415
Gherardo	416
Ghert	417
Ghes	418
Ghey	419
Ghez	421
Ghi	422
Ghid	423
Ghil	424
Ghir	425
Ghis	426
Ghisli	427
Ghosal	427
Ghose	427
Ghoshal	427
Ghuman	427
Ghurye	427
Gi	428
Giac	429
Gial	431
Giam	432
Gian	433
Gianno	434
Giar	435
Giat	436
Gib	437
Gibb	437
Gibbe	438
Gibbo	439
Gibbons	441
Gibbs	442
Gibbs, H.	443
Gibbs, S.	444
Gibe	445
Gibi	446
Gibn	447
Gibs	448

Gibson	449	Gillett	479	Giraul	523
Gibson, H.	449	Gilli	481	Gird	524
Gibson, S.	451	Gillm	482	Girdhari	524
Gic	452	Gillo	483	Girglani	524
Gid	453	Gills	484	Giri	525
Gidwani	453	Gilly	485	Giriappa	525
Gie	454	Gilm	486	Girish	525
Gies	455	Gilman	487	Girja	525
Gif	456	Gilmo	488	Girl	525
Giffe	457	Gilp	489	Girmaji	525
Giffo	458	Gim	491	Giro	526
Gig	459	Gin	492	Giron	527
Gigo	461	Gino	493	Girou	528
Gih	462	Ginsberg	493	Girt	529
Gil	463	Gio	494	Gis	531
Gilani	463	Giof	495	Gise	532
Gilbert	464	Giol	496	Gisl	533
Gilbert, J.	465	Gior	497	Gism	534
Gilbert, S.	466	Giorg	498	Giso	535
Gilc	467	Giorgio	499	Git	536
Gild	468	Giot	511	Gita	536
Gildo	469	Giov	512	Giu	537
Gile	471	Giove	513	Gius	538
Giles	472	Giovi	514	Giv	539
Gilf	473	Gir	515	Gl	541
Gili	474	Giral	516	Glad	542
Gill	475	Girar	517	Glads	543
Gille	476	Girard, M.	518	Glai	544
Gilles	477	Girarde	519	Glan	545
Gillesp	478	Girardi	521	Glanv	546
Gillet	479	Girau	522	Glap	547

Glas	548
Glass	549
Glau	551
Glauc	552
Glaz	553
Gle	554
Gled	555
Glei	556
Gleig	557
Glen	558
Gli	559
Glin	561
Glo	562
Glob	562
Glos	563
Glossary	563
Glou	564
Glov	565
Glover	566
Glu	567
Gly	568
Gm	569
Gn	571
Gnanam	571
Gni	572
Gno	572
Go	573
Goa	573
Gob	574
Gobi	575
Gobind	575
Goc	576
God	577
Godbole	577
Godd	578
Gode	579
Godef	581
Godes	582
Godf	583
Godi	584
Godin	585
Godk	586
Godm	587
Godman	587
Godo	588
Godon	589
Godrej	589
Godse	589
Godw	591
Godwin	592
Godwin, M.	592
Goe	593
Goed	594
Goel	595
Goenka	595
Goep	596
Goer	597
Goes	598
Goet	599
Goetz	611
Gof	612
Gog	613
Gogna	613
Gogvi	613
Goh	614
Gohain	614
Gohil	614
Goi	615
Gois	616
Gokak	616
Gokhale	616
Gol	617
Gold	618
Golden	618
Goldi	619
Goldins	619
Goldman	619
Goldo	621
Golds	622
Goldsc	623
Goldsm	624
Goldsmith	624
Goldstein	624
Goldy	624
Gole	625
Goli	626
Golo	627
Golov	628
Golt	629
Golwala	629
Golwalkar	629
Gom	631
Gomango	631

Gombe	632	Google	658	Goss	677
Gome	633	Gook	659	Gosse	678
Gomes	633	Goon	659	Gossel	679
Gomez	633	Goonatilake	659	Gosso	681
Gomm	634	Gopa	659	Gost	682
Gon	635	Gopal	659	Goswami	682
Gond	636	Gopalachari	659	Goswamy	682
Gonda	636	Gopalakrishna	659	Got	683
Gondi	637	Gopalan	659	Goth	684
Gone	638	Gopi	659	Gott	685
Gonn	639	Gopinath	659	Gotti	686
Gonsalves	639	Gor	661	Gotts	687
Gont	641	Gora	661	Gou	688
Gonz	642	Gorakh	661	Gouf	689
Gonzal	643	Gorden	661	Goug	691
Goo	644	Gordon	662	Gough	692
Gooc	645	Gordon, G.	663	Gouj	693
Gooch	645	Gordon, M.	664	Goul	694
Good	646	Gordon, S.	665	Goulb	695
Goode	647	Gore	666	Gould	696
Goodel	648	Gorg	667	Gould, J.	697
Gooden	649	Gorh	668	Gould, S.	698
Goodf	651	Gori	669	Gouls	699
Goodh	652	Gorm	671	Goun	711
Goodm	653	Goro	672	Goup	712
Goodman	653	Gorr	673	Gour	713
Goodr	654	Gors	674	Gour	715
Goodrich, M.	655	Gort	675	Gourd	714
Goodw	656	Gos	676	Gourg	715
Goodwin, M.	657	Gosain	676	Gourl	716
Goody	658	Gosal	676	Gous	717

Gout	718
Gouv	719
Gov	721
Goverdhan	721
Govern	721
Governov	721
Govil	721
Govinda	721
Gow	722
Gowda	722
Gower	723
Goy	724
Goyal	724
Goz	725
Gr	726
Grab	727
Graber	728
Grac	729
Grace	729
Graci	731
Grad	732
Grado	733
Grae	734
Graes	735
Graf	736
Graft	737
Grah	738
Graham, G.	739
Graham, M.	741
Graham, S.	742
Grahm	742
Grai	743
Gral	744
Gram	745
Grammo	746
Gramo	747
Gran	748
Granc	749
Grand	751
Grandes	752
Grandi	753
Grandm	754
Grandv	755
Grane	756
Grang	757
Granger	758
Grani	759
Grant	761
Grant, H.	762
Grant, S.	763
Grantl	764
Grants	764
Granv	765
Grap	766
Gras	767
Grass	768
Grassi	769
Grat	771
Grati	772
Gratt	773
Grau	774
Grav	775
Graves	776
Gravi	777
Gray	778
Gray, G.	779
Gray, M.	781
Gray, S.	782
Gray, W.	783
Grays	784
Graz	785
Grdsman	785
Gre	786
Great	786
Greav	787
Greb	788
Grec	789
Greco	791
Gred	792
Gree	793
Greel	794
Green	795
Green, G.	796
Green, M.	797
Green, S.	798
Greene	799
Greene, J.	811
Greene, S.	812
Greenh	813
Greeno	815
Greenol	814
Greenw	816
Gref	817

Greg	818	Griffin	851	Grov	883
Gregg	819	Griffin, M.	852	Grover	884
Gregori	821	Griffith	853	Groves	884
Gregory	822	Griffith, M.	854	Gru	885
Gregory, M.	823	Griffiths	855	Grue	886
Grei	824	Griffo	856	Grul	887
Grel	825	Grig	857	Grun	888
Gren	826	Gril	858	Grund	889
Greni	827	Grillo	859	Grune	891
Grenv	828	Grim	861	Grup	892
Grep	829	Grime	862	Grut	893
Gres	831	Grimk	863	Gry	894
Gress	832	Grimm	864	Gryp	895
Gresw	833	Grimo	865	Gu	896
Gret	834	Grin	866	Guad	897
Gretto	835	Grinr	867	Guai	898
Greu	836	Grins	868	Gual	899
Grev	837	Gris	869	Guald	911
Grevi	838	Grism	869	Gualt	912
Grevy	839	Grisw	871	Guan	913
Grew	841	Griv	872	Guar	914
Grewal	841	Gro	873	Guari	915
Grey	842	Groe	874	Guarn	916
Grey, G.	843	Grol	875	Guas	917
Grey, M.	844	Gron	876	Guat	918
Grey, S.	845	Gros	877	Guaz	919
Gri	846	Gross	878	Gub	922
Grid	847	Grosv	879	Gud	922
Grie	848	Grot	881	Gudm	923
Grierson	848	Grou	882	Gue	924
Grif	849	Group	882	Guel	925

Guen	926
Gueno	927
Guep	928
Guer	929
Guere	931
Guern	933
Guerol	932
Guerr	934
Guerri	935
Gues	936
Guct	937
Gueu	938
Guev	939
Guf	941
Gug	942
Guha	942
Gui	943
Guib	944
Guic	945
Guid	946
Guide	946
Guidi	947
Guido	948
Guie	949
Guig	951
Guij	952
Guil	953
Guild	954
Guild, M.	955
Guile	956
Guill	957
Guille	958
Guilli	959
Guillo	961
Guillot	962
Guim	963
Guin	964
Guir	965
Guis	966
Guise	967
Guit	968
Guiz	969
Gujarat	969
Gujrel	969
Gul	971
Gulati	971
Gulg	972
Gull	973
Gulshan	973
Gulzar	973
Gum	974
Gun	975
Gunn	976
Gunt	977
Gunther	977
Gupta	977
Gupte	977
Gur	978
Gurbachan	978
Gurcharan	978
Gurdev	978
Gure	979
Guria	979
Gurjas	979
Gurjeet	979
Gurmit	979
Gurn	981
Gurnam	981
Gurpreet	981
Gursharan	981
Gurtej	981
Guru	981
Gurudev	981
Gurumurthy	981
Guruswamy	981
Gus	982
Gut	983
Guth	984
Gutt	985
Guy	986
Guyar	987
Guye	988
Guyer	989
Guyo	989
Guys	991
Guyt	992
Guz	993
Gw	994
Gwy	995
Gy	996
Gyan	996
Gyatso	996
Gyll	997

Gys	998
Gyz	999

H

Ha	111
Haas	112
Hab	113
Haber	114
Habert	115
Habi	116
Habib	116
Hac	117
Hack	118
Hacket	119
Hackett	121
Hackl	122
Hackm	123
Haco	124
Had	125
Hadd	126
Haddo	127
Hade	128
Haden	128
Hadf	129
Hadl	131
Hadr	132
Hae	133
Hael	134
Haen	135
Haer	136
Haeu	137
Haf	138
Hafi	139
Hag	141
Hagem	142
Hagen	143
Hager	144
Hagg	145
Hags	146
Hagu	147
Hague	147
Hah	148
Hai	149
Hail	151
Hain	152
Haines	153
Haj	154
Hajela	154
Hajra	154
Hak	155
Hakam	155
Hakim	155
Hakl	156
Haksavr	156
Hal	157
Halappa	157
Hald	158
Haldar	158
Halde	159
Hale	161
Hale, G.	162
Hale, M.	163
Hale, S.	164
Hale, W.	165
Halen	166
Hales	167
Halet	168
Half	169
Halh	171
Hali	172
Halif	173
Halim	173
Hall	174
Hall	174
Hall, D.	175
Hall, G.	176
Hall, J.	177
Hall, M.	178
Hall, S.	179
Hall, W.	181
Hallam	182
Halle	183
Hallec	184
Haller	185
Hallet	186
Halley	187
Halli	188
Hallig	189
Halliw	191
Hallo	192
Hallow	193
Halm	194
Halp	195
Hals	196

Halsan	196
Halt	197
Ham	198
Hamb	199
Hamd	211
Hamdard	211
Hame	212
Hameed	212
Hameli	213
Hamer	214
Hamert	215
Hamesh	215
Hami	216
Hamid	216
Hamil	217
Hamilton	218
Hamilton, G.	218
Hamilton, M.	219
Hamilton, S.	221
Hamilton, W.	222
Haml	223
Hamm	224
Hammo	225
Hammond, G.	226
Hammond, M.	227
Hamo	228
Hamp	229
Hamps	231
Hampt	232
Hamy	229
Han	233
Hanc	234
Hancock, M.	235
Hand	236
Handa	236
Handbook	236
Handoo	236
Hane	237
Hanf	238
Hang	239
Hangal	239
Hangloo	239
Hanif	239
Hank	241
Hanm	242
Hann	243
Hanne	244
Hanni	245
Hanno	246
Hano	247
Hanr	248
Hans	249
Hansen	249
Hanso	251
Hanuman	251
Hanumantha	251
Hanw	252
Haq	253
Haque	253
Har	254
Haran	254
Harari	254
Harb	255
Harbaksh	255
Harbans	255
Harc	256
Harcharan	256
Harcou	257
Hard	258
Hardas	258
Harden	259
Harder	259
Hardi	261
Hardie	262
Harding	263
Hardinge	264
Hardo	265
Hardt	266
Hardw	267
Hardy	268
Hardy, G.	269
Hardy, M.	271
Hardy, S.	272
Hardy, W.	273
Hare	274
Hare, M.	275
Haren	276
Harew	277
Harf	278
Harg	279
Hargopal	279
Hari	281
Haridas	261

Hariharan	281	Harris, S.	316	Hasel	347
Harikishan	281	Harris, W.	317	Hasen	348
Hario	282	Harrison	318	Hashmi	348
Harish	282	Harrison, F.	319	Hasija	348
Hariyana	282	Harrison, M.	321	Hask	349
Harl	283	Harrison, S.	322	Haski	351
Harle	284	Harrison, W.	323	Hasl	352
Harley	285	Hars	324	Hasnain	352
Harlo	286	Harsh	324	Hasrat	352
Harm	287	Hart	325	Hass	353
Harmo	288	Hart, M.	326	Hasse	354
Harn	289	Harte	327	Hassel	355
Harnam	289	Harte, M.	328	Hast	356
Harni	291	Harti	329	Hastings	357
Haro	292	Hartl	331	Hastings, M.	358
Haroon	292	Hartley	332	Hasw	359
Harp	293	Hartm	333	Hat	361
Harpal	293	Harto	334	Hatf	362
Harper	294	Harts	335	Hath	363
Harper, G.	294	Hartu	336	Hathert	364
Harper, W.	295	Hartw	337	Hathi	364
Harpreel	295	Hartz	338	Hats	365
Harr	296	Harv	339	Hatt	366
Harri	297	Harvard	339	Hatz	367
Harriman, M.	298	Harvey	341	Hau	368
Harrin	299	Harvey, M.	342	Hauf	369
Harrington, M.	311	Harw	343	Haug	371
Harrio	312	Haryana	343	Haul	372
Harris	313	Has	344	Haun	373
Harris, F.	314	Hasd	345	Haup	374
Harris, M.	315	Hase	346	Haur	375

Haus	376	Hayes, M.	418	Heber	445
Hauss	377	Hayg	419	Hebert	446
Hausso	378	Hayl	421	Hec	447
Haut	379	Haym	422	Heck	448
Hautem	381	Hayn	423	Hecker	449
Hautp	382	Haynes	424	Hect	451
Hav	383	Hays	425	Hed	452
Havel	384	Hayt	426	Hedg	453
Havell	384	Hayw	427	Hedi	454
Haven	385	Haz	428	Hedl	455
Haven, M.	386	Hazara	428	Hedo	456
Haver	387	Hazari	428	Hedw	457
Havi	388	Hazarika	428	Hee	458
Haw	389	Haze	429	Heehs	458
Hawes	391	Hazel	429	Heer	459
Hawk	392	Hazl	431	Hef	461
Hawkins	393	Hazra	431	Heg	462
Hawkins, M.	394	Hd	431	Hegde	462
Hawks	395	He	432	Heges	463
Hawl	396	Headl	433	Hegh	464
Hawo	397	Heal	434	Hei	465
Haws	398	Hear	435	Heil	466
Hawt	399	Hearn	436	Heim	467
Hax	411	Heat	437	Hein	468
Hay	412	Heath	437	Heinr	469
Hay, M.	413	Heath, M.	438	Heins	471
Hayden	414	Heathc	439	Heinz	472
Hayden, M.	415	Heathe	441	Heis	473
Haydon	416	Heato	442	Hel	474
Haye	417	Heb	443	Heli	475
Hayes	418	Heben	444	Hell	476

Helle	477	Henry	521	Hermo	555
Helm	478	Henry, M.	523	Hermon	556
Helmh	479	Henry, S.	524	Hern	557
Helmo	481	Henry, W.	525	Hernd	558
Helo	482	Henry,G	522	Hero	559
Help	483	Hens	526	Herol	561
Helps	484	Hent	527	Heron	562
Helson	484	Hentz	528	Herp	563
Helv	485	Hep	529	Herr	564
Helw	486	Her	531	Herrer	565
Hem	487	Herar	532	Herri	566
Heme	488	Herau	533	Herrin	567
Hemm	489	Herb	534	Herrm	568
Hemp	491	Herber	535	Hers	569
Hems	492	Herbert	536	Hersc	571
Hen	493	Herbert, M.	537	Herse	572
Henc	494	Herbi	538	Hert	573
Hend	495	Herc	539	Hertf	574
Henderson	496	Herd	541	Herts	575
Henderson, M.	497	Here	542	Hertz	576
Hendr	498	Hereu	543	Herv	577
Henf	499	Herf	544	Hervey	578
Heng	511	Herg	545	Hervey, M.	579
Henk	512	Heri	546	Herw	581
Henkel	513	Herio	547	Herz	582
Henl	514	Heris	548	Hes	583
Henn	515	Herl	549	Hese	584
Henni	516	Herm	551	Hesm	585
Hennin	517	Hermann	552	Hess	586
Henr	518	Herme	553	Hesse	587
Henrio	519	Hermi	554	Hest	588

Het	589
Hett	591
Heu	592
Heum	593
Heur	594
Heus	595
Hev	596
Hew	597
Hewe	598
Hewi	599
Hewit	611
Hewl	612
Hews	613
Hex	614
Hey	615
Heyf	616
Heyl	617
Heym	618
Heyn	619
Heys	621
Heyw	622
Hi	623
Hib	624
Hibo	625
Hic	626
Hick	627
Hicke	628
Hicko	629
Hicks	631
Hid	632
Hidayatullah	632
Hie	633
Hig	634
Higen	634
Higg	635
Higgins	636
Higginson	637
High	638
Hij	639
Hil	641
Hilary	641
Hild	642
Hilder	643
Hildr	644
Hill	645
Hill, G.	646
Hill, M.	647
Hill, S.	648
Hilla	649
Hille	651
Hiller	652
Hillh	653
Hilli	654
Hills	655
Hilt	656
Hilton	656
Him	657
Himachal	657
Himalya	657
Himat	657
Himaye	657
Himi	658
Hin	659
Hincks	661
Hind	662
Hindi	662
Hindu	662
Hindustan	662
Hing	663
Hingorani	663
Hino	663
Hinr	664
Hins	665
Hint	666
Hip	667
Hir	668
Hira	668
Hiremash	668
Hiremath	668
Hiro	668
Hirs	669
Hirt	671
Hirway	671
Hirz	672
His	673
History	673
Hit	674
Hitchi	675
Hitkari	675
Hitt	676
Hj	677
Ho	678
Hoar	679

Hob	681	Hok	721	Holmes, M.	752
Hobb	682	Hol	722	Holmes, S.	753
Hobh	683	Holb	723	Holo	754
Hobhods	684	Holbr	724	Holr	755
Hobs	684	Holc	725	Hols	756
Hoc	685	Hold	726	Holste	757
Hocq	686	Holden	726	Holt	758
Hod	687	Holder	727	Holw	759
Hodg	688	Holds	728	Holy	761
Hodges, M.W	689	Hole	729	Holz	762
Hodgs	691	Holg	731	Hom	763
Hods	692	Holi	732	Homb	764
Hodson	692	Holl	733	Home	765
Hoe	693	Holland	734	Homer	766
Hoel	694	Holland, G.	735	Homes	767
Hoes	695	Holland, M.	736	Homm	768
Hoet	695	Holland, S.	737	Hon	769
Hoey	696	Hollande	737	Hond	771
Hof	697	Holley	738	Hone	772
Hoff	698	Holli	739	Hong	772
Hoffm	699	Hollin	741	Honi	773
Hoffman	711	Hollis	742	Hono	774
Hoffman, M.	711	Hollis, M.	743	Hont	775
Hofl	712	Hollist	744	Hoo	776
Hofm	713	Hollo	745	Hood, M.	777
Hog	714	Holly	746	Hooda	777
Hogar	715	Holm	747	Hoof	778
Hogg	716	Holm	747	Hoog	779
Hoh	717	Holme	748	Hooja	779
Hohenl	718	Holmes	749	Hook	781
Hohenz	719	Holmes, G.	751	Hooke	782

Hooker	783	Horw	824	Howard, W.	853
Hooker, M.	784	Hos	825	Howd	854
Hoon	784	Hosain	825	Howe	855
Hoop	785	Hosan	825	Howe, G.	856
Hooper, G.	786	Hosk	826	Howe, M.	857
Hooper, M.	787	Hosm	827	Howe, S.	858
Hooper, S.	788	Hosp	828	Howel	859
Hoor	789	Hoss	829	Howi	861
Hop	791	Host	831	Howis	862
Hope	791	Hot	832	Howit	863
Hopf	792	Hotel	832	Howl	864
Hopk	793	Hotm	833	Howle	865
Hopkins, G.	794	Hott	834	Hows	866
Hopkins, M.	795	Hou	835	Hox	866
Hopkins, S.	796	Houd	836	Hoy	867
Hopkinson	797	Houe	837	Hoyt	868
Hopp	798	Houg	838	Hoyt, M.	869
Hoppins	798	Houn	839	Hoz	872
Hopt	799	Hour	841	Hr	873
Hor	811	Hous	842	Hu	874
Horl	812	House	842	Hub	875
Horn	813	Houst	843	Hubbard, M.	876
Hornb	814	Houston	843	Hube	877
Horne	815	Hout	844	Hubert	878
Horner	816	Hov	845	Hubn	879
Hors	817	Hovey	846	Hubs	881
Horsl	818	How	847	Huc	882
Horst	819	Howard	848	Hud	883
Hort	821	Howard, G.	849	Huddl	884
Horten	822	Howard, M.	851	Huds	885
Horto	823	Howard, S.	852	Hudson, M.	886

Hue	887	Humphreys	927	Hurd, M.	961
Huet	888	Humphri	928	Hurdi	962
Huf	889	Humps	929	Hure	963
Hug	891	Hun	931	Huri	964
Hugh	892	Hunc	932	Hurl	965
Hughes	893	Hund	933	Hurls	966
Hughes, M.	894	Hune	934	Hurt	967
Hugo	895	Hunf	935	Hus	968
Hugon	896	Hung	936	Husain	968
Hugu	897	Huni	937	Huse	969
Hugui	898	Hunn	938	Husk	971
Hui	899	Hunt	939	Huss	972
Huit	911	Hunt, G.	941	Hut	973
Hukam	911	Hunt, M.	942	Hutchins	974
Hul	912	Hunt, S.	943	Hutchinson	975
Hull	913	Hunte	944	Hutchinson, G.	976
Hulli	914	Hunter	945	Hutchinson, M.	977
Hulm	915	Hunter, M.	946	Hutchinson, S.	978
Hulo	916	Hunter, S.	947	Huth	979
Huls	917	Hunting	948	Huti	981
Hum	918	Huntington	949	Hutt	982
Human	918	Huntington, G.	951	Hutter	983
Humayun	918	Huntington, M.	952	Hutto	984
Humb	919	Huntington, S.	953	Hutton	985
Hume	921	Huntl	954	Hutton, M.	985
Hume, M.	922	Hunto	955	Hux	986
Humf	923	Hunts	956	Huxley	986
Humi	924	Huo	957	Huy	987
Humm	925	Hup	958	Huys	988
Hump	926	Huq	958	Huz	989
Humphrey	926	Hur	959	Hw	991

Hy	992	Ili	28	Ingi	49
Hyde	993	Ill	29	Ingl	51
Hyde, H.	994	Im	31	Ingli	52
Hyde, P.	995	Imam	31	Ingo	53
Hydra	995	Imb	32	Ingr	54
Hyl	996	Iml	33	Ingre	55
Hyn	997	Immanuel	33	Ini	56
Hyp	998	Imp	34	Inm	57
Hyr	999	Imperial	34	Inn	58
I		Imran	33	Innaiah	58
Ia	11	Imran	34	Ins	59
Iabal	11	Imtiaz	34	Institute	59
Ib	12	In	35	Int	61
IBM	12	Inamdar	35	International	61
Ibn	13	Inc	36	Inv	62
Ibr	14	Inch	37	Inw	63
Ibrahim	14	Ind	38	Io	64
Ic	15	Inder	38	Ir	65
Ich	16	Indi	39	Iram	65
Ick	17	India	39	Iran	65
Id	18	Indian	39	Irani	65
Ide	19	Indira	39	Iraq	65
Ido	21	Indo	41	Irel	65
Ie	22	Indra	41	Iren	66
Ienger	22	Indu	42	Iret	67
If	23	Inf	43	Irfan	67
Ig	24	Ing	44	Iri	68
Ih	25	Inge	45	Irl	69
Ijari	25	Ingel	46	Iro	71
Ik	26	Inger	47	Irshad	71
Il	27	Ingh	48	Irv	72

Irwin	72
Is	73
Isaac	73
Isab	74
Isam	75
Isar	76
Isc	77
Ise	78
Ish	79
Ishwar	79
Isi	81
Isl	82
Islam	82
Ism	83
Isn	84
Iso	85
Iss	86
Ist	87
Iswaran	87
It	88
Italy	88
Ith	89
Itt	91
Iu	92
Iv	93
Ive	94
Ives	95
Ivo	96
Ivy	96
Ix	97
Iyengar	97
Iyer	97
Iz	98
Izm	99

J

Ja	11
Jac	12
Jack	12
Jackson	13
Jackson, J.	13
Jackson, S.	14
Jaco	15
Jacob	15
Jacobi	16
Jacobs	17
Jacop	18
Jacq	19
Jacqui	21
Jadav	21
Jadeja	21
Jadhav	21
Jae	22
Jaf	23
Jafa	23
Jaffar	23
Jag	24
Jagannath	24
Jagat	24
Jagdev	24
Jagdish	24
Jaggi	24
Jagjit	24
Jagjiwan	24
Jagmohan	24
Jagtar	24
Jah	25
Jahangir	25
Jai	25
Jaidev	25
Jaidka	25
Jain	25
Jainendra	25
Jaini	25
Jaipal	25
Jaipur	25
Jaiswal	25
Jaitly	25
Jakhar	25
Jal	26
Jalal	26
Jalan	26
Jalandhar	26
Jallunder	26
Jalota	26
Jam	27
Jamal	27
James	28
James, M.	28
James, S.	29
Jameso	31
Jami	32
Jamia	32
Jamil	32

Jammu	32
Jamna	32
Jamshed	32
Jamwal	32
Jan	33
Janaki	33
Janala	33
Janardhan	33
Jane	33
Jangam	33
Jangir	33
Jani	33
Jann	34
Jans	35
Janta	35
Japan	35
Jaq	36
Jar	37
Jariwala	37
Jarnail	37
Jarv	38
Jas	39
Jasbir	39
Jash	39
Jasjit	39
Jasmer	39
Jasmine	39
Jaspal	39
Jaswal	39
Jaswant	39
Jat	39
Jatava	39
Jatinder	39
Jatti	39
Jau	41
Jauhar	41
Javed	41
Jawahar	41
Jawed	41
Jay	42
Jayadeva	42
Jayakar	42
Jayal	42
Jayandra	42
Jayant	42
Jayaraj	42
Jayaram	42
Jayaswal	42
Je	43
Jean	43
Jeb	44
Jcclani	44
Jeevan	44
Jef	45
Jefferson	45
Jeffre	46
Jeffrey	46
Jeffri	47
Jem	49
Jen	51
Jena	51
Jenk	52
Jenks	53
Jenn	54
Jer	55
Jero	56
Jerv	57
Jes	58
Jetha	58
Jethmalani	58
Jethwani	58
Jevons	58
Jew	59
Jewel	59
Jey	59
Jha	59
Jhabvala	59
Jhanji	59
Jhar	59
Jhaveri	59
Jhingan	59
Jhingran	59
Ji	61
Jig	61
Jina	61
Jinah	61
Jindal	61
Jinnah	61
Jitender	61
Jo	62
Joad	62
Job	62
Joc	63

Jodh	63
Joe	64
Jog	64
Joginder	64
Joh	65
Johar	65
Johl	65
John	65
Johnso	66
Johnson	66
Johnson, G.	67
Johnson, M.	68
Johnson, S.	69
Johnson, W.	71
Johnst	72
Johnston, M.	73
Johr	73
Johri	73
Joi	74
Jol	75
Jolly	75
Jon	76
Jones	76
Jones, G.	77
Jones, M.	78
Jones, S.	79
Jons	81
Joor	81
Jor	82
Jordan	82
Jorge	82
Jos	83
Jose	83
Joseph	83
Josh	83
Joshi	83
Joss	84
Jot	85
Joti	85
Jotwani	85
Jou	86
Joud	86
Journal	86
Jow	87
Joy	88
Joyc	89
Ju	91
Jud	92
Judas	92
Judge	92
Juds	93
Juesawala	93
Jug	93
Jul	94
Julka	94
Juma	94
Jun	95
Juneja	95
Jung	95
Jus	96
Justice	96
Justin	96
Juv	97
Jux	98
Jy	99
Jyoti	99

K

Ka	11
Kabir	11
Kabra	11
Kachroo	11
Kachru	11
Kadam	11
Kadir	11
Kagzi	11
Kah	12
Kahan	12
Kahlon	12
Kai	13
Kaimal	13
Kainth	13
Kaj	13
Kak	13
Kakar	13
Kakkar	13
Kal	14
Kala	14
Kalabagh	14
Kalam	14
Kale	14
Kalekar	14
Kalhan	14
Kali	14

Kalia	14	Kani	16	Karl	18
Kalian	14	Kanji	16	Karlikar	18
Kalidas	14	Kankachary	16	Karma	15
Kalim	14	Kanna	16	Karma	18
Kalki	14	Kannada	16	Karn	18
Kalla	14	Kannan	16	Karnad	18
Kalpana	14	Kannu	16	Karnatka	18
Kalra	14	Kanongo	16	Karpov	18
Kalsi	14	Kansal	16	Kartar	18
Kalyan	14	Kanshi	16	Karthiklyan	18
Kam	15	Kant	16	Karuna	18
Kamal	15	Kanth	16	Karunakaran	18
Kamaluddin	15	Kanwal	16	Karunanidhi	18
Kamalvijayan	15	Kanwar	16	Karve	18
Kamat	15	Kao	16	Kas	19
Kamble	15	Kap	17	Kashi	19
Kamboj	15	Kapadia	17	Kashmir	19
Kameshwar	15	Kapil	17	Kashyap	19
Kami	15	Kapila	17	Kasim	19
Kamla	15	Kaplan	17	Kasliwal	19
Kamlapati	15	Kapoor	17	Kasturi	19
Kamt	15	Kapur	17	Kataria	19
Kan	16	Kar	18	Kathm	19
Kanal	16	Karan	18	Kathpal	19
Kanan	16	Karandikar	18	Kathuria	19
Kanchan	16	Karanja	18	Katiyar	19
Kanda	16	Karanth	18	Katju	19
Kandel	16	Karim	18	Katyal	19
Kandey	16	Karin	18	Kau	21
Kane	16	Karkare	18	Kaul	21
Kang	16	Karkel	18	Kaur	21

Name	Number
Kaushal	21
Kaushik	21
Kaveri	21
Kaviraj	21
Kaw	22
Kawatra	22
Kay	23
Kayastha	23
Kaye	23
Kazi	23
Kazmi	23
Ke	24
Keat	25
Keay	25
Kedar	25
Kedia	25
Kee	26
Keen	26
Keer	26
Kehar	26
Kei	27
Keith	28
Kel	29
Kelkar	29
Keller	29
Kelley	29
Kellogg	29
Kelly	29
Kem	31
Kemp	32
Ken	33
Kend	33
Kenn	34
Kennedy	35
Kennedy, M.	36
Kent	37
Kep	38
Ker	39
Kerala	39
Kerr	41
Kes	42
Kesar	42
Kesarwani	42
Kesava	42
Kesavan	42
Keswani	42
Ket	43
Ketkar	43
Kewal	43
Key	44
Kh	45
Khadi	45
Khadilkar	45
Khair	45
Khaitan	45
Khajan	45
Khajuria	45
Khalid	45
Khalifa	45
Khalsa	45
Khan	45
Khanna	45
Kharbanda	45
Khare	45
Kharrla	45
Khasi	45
Khati	45
Khatre	45
Khatt	45
Khazam	45
Khazan	45
Kher	45
Khes	45
Khetan	45
Khilani	45
Khochar	45
Khokar	45
Khote	45
Khullar	45
Khumble	45
Khunda	45
Khurana	45
Khurmi	45
Khurshid	45
Khushwant	45
Khusro	45
Khwaja	45
Khyal	45
Ki	46
Kicker	46
Kidwai	46
Kie	47
Kil	48

Kim	49	Knight, M-Z	71	Kort	85
Kin	51	Kno	72	Kos	86
Kincaid	51	Know	73	Kosambi	86
Kincail	51	Knox	74	Koser	86
King	52	Ko	75	Kosh	86
King, J.	53	Koc	76	Kosla	86
King, P.	54	Kochar	76	Kot	87
Kings	55	Kochhar	76	Koteshwar	87
Kins	56	Kodaikanal	76	Kothari	87
Kip	57	Koe	77	Koti	87
Kir	58	Koen	78	Kotpal	87
Kiran	58	Koh	79	Kotwal	87
Kirk	59	Kohima	79	Kou	88
Kirloskar	59	Kohlapur	81	Koufman	88
Kirmani	59	Kohli	79	Koul	88
Kirpa	59	Koilpillai	79	Kovind	88
Kirpal	59	Koirala	79	Kr	89
Kirs	61	Kokaje	79	Krau	91
Kirti	61	Kol	81	Kre	92
Kirtikar	61	Kolasa	81	Kripa	92
Kishore	61	Kolkata	81	Kripal	92
Kishwar	61	Komal	81	Kriplani	92
Kit	62	Kon	82	Krishan	92
Kl	63	Koner	82	Krishna	92
Klein	64	Konnur	82	Krishnan	92
Kli	65	Konrad	82	Krist	92
Klo	66	Kool	82	Kro	93
Kn	67	Kop	83	Kru	94
Kne	68	Kor	84	Ku	95
Kni	69	Korer	84	Kuber	95
Knight, A-L	71	Kores	84	Kuh	96

Kuldeep	96
Kuldip	96
Kulkarni	96
Kulke	96
Kulpati	96
Kulshrestha	96
Kulsrestha	96
Kulveer	96
Kulwant	96
Kulwinder	96
Kumar	96
Kumarappa	96
Kumran	96
Kumria	96
Kumu	96
Kundra	96
Kundu	96
Kundu	96
Kupuswami	96
Kureshi	96
Kurian	96
Kurukshetra	96
Kurup	96
Kus	97
Kushwaha	97
Kusum	97
Kuthalia	97
Kutt	97
Kutty	97
Kw	98
Kwatra	98
Kwoon	98
Ky	99
Kyle	99

L

La	111
Lab	112
Labar	113
Labat	114
Labbe	115
Labe	116
Labeo	117
Labh	117
Labi	118
Labil	119
Labl	121
Labo	122
Labor	123
Labou	124
Labour	125
Labr	126
Labru	127
Lac	128
Lacam	129
Lace	131
Lach	132
Lachap	133
Lachas	134
Lachat	135
Lachau	136
Lache	137
Lachm	138
Laci	139
Lack	141
Laco	142
Lacor	143
Lacos	144
Lacou	145
Lacr	146
Lacro	147
Lacros	148
Lacru	149
Lact	151
Lacy	152
Lad	153
Ladakh	153
Ladbeaker	153
Ladd	154
Ladi	155
Lado	156
Ladr	157
Lae	158
Laf	159
Lafay	161
Lafe	162
Laff	163
Lafl	164
Lafo	165
Lafont	166
Lafor	167
Lafos	168
Lafr	169
Lafu	171

Lag	172	Lali	195	Lamot	235
Lagar	173	Lall	196	Lamou	236
Lage	174	Lalle	197	Lamp	237
Laghu	174	Lalli	198	Lampi	238
Lagi	175	Lallo	199	Lampr	239
Lagn	176	Lally	211	Lams	241
Lago	177	Lalo	212	Lamy	242
Lagr	178	Laloo	212	Lan	243
Lagre	179	Lalvani	212	Lanc	244
Lagu	181	Lalwani	212	Lancaster, M.	245
Lagui	182	Lam	213	Lance	246
Lah	183	Lama	213	Lancel	247
Lahiri	183	Laman	214	Lancey	248
Laho	184	Lamar	215	Lanci	249
Lahul	184	Lamarm	216	Lanco	251
Lai	185	Lamart	217	Lancr	252
Lain	186	Lamb	218	Land	253
Laing	187	Lamba	219	Lande	254
Lair	188	Lambe	221	Lander	255
Lais	189	Lambert	222	Landes	256
Laj	191	Lamberti	223	Landi	257
Lajpat	191	Lambi	224	Lando	258
Lak	192	Lambo	225	Landon	259
Lakdawala	192	Lambr	226	Landor	261
Lakhan	192	Lambt	227	Landr	262
Lakhotia	192	Lame	228	Lands	263
Lakshman	193	Lamet	229	Landu	264
Lakshmanarayan	192	Lami	231	Lane	265
Lakshmi	192	Lamir	232	Lane, M.	266
Lal	193	Lamo	233	Laneh	267
Lalann	194	Lamon	234	Lanf	268

Lang	269	Lapi	313	Lasse	347
Lang, M.	271	Lapl	314	Lassu	348
Langd	272	Lapo	315	Last	349
Langdo	273	Lapp	316	Lat	351
Lange	274	Lapr	317	Lath	352
Langen	275	Lar	318	Lathr	353
Langer	276	Larc	319	Lathrop, G.	354
Langet	277	Lard	321	Lathrop, M.	355
Langf	278	Larg	322	Lati	356
Langh	279	Lari	323	Latif	356
Langi	281	Lark	324	Latim	357
Langl	282	Larn	325	Lato	358
Langle	283	Laro	326	Latour	359
Langlo	284	Larochef	327	Latourr	361
Langr	285	Larochej	328	Latr	362
Langridge	285	Larom	329	Latri	363
Langt	286	Laron	331	Latro	364
Langu	287	Larou	332	Lattel	364
Lanj	288	Larr	333	Latu	365
Lank	289	Larri	334	Lau	366
Lanm	291	Lart	335	Laud	367
Lann	292	Laru	336	Laude	368
Lano	293	Las	337	Lauderd	369
Lans	294	Lasal	338	Laudi	371
Lansd	295	Lasan	339	Laudo	372
Lant	296	Lasc	341	Lauf	373
Lanz	297	Lasco	342	Laug	374
Lao	298	Lase	343	Laum	375
Lap	299	Lasi	344	Laun	376
Lape	311	Lask	345	Laur	377
Laph	312	Lass	346	Laure	378

Laurenc	379	Lawrence, S.	423	Lebret	452
Laurens	381	Lawrence, W.	424	Lebri	453
Laurent	382	Laws	425	Lebru	454
Laurenti	383	Laxman	425	Lec	455
Lauri	384	Laxmi	425	Lecar	456
Laurie	385	Lay	426	Lecc	457
Lauris	386	Layc	427	Lech	458
Lauro	387	Layn	428	Leche	459
Laus	388	Layt	429	Leck	461
Laut	389	Laz	431	Lecl	462
Lauv	391	Lazarus	431	Leclu	463
Lav	392	Lazz	432	Leco	464
Lavale	393	Le	433	Lecom	465
Lavall	394	Leac	434	Lecon	466
Lavalli	395	Leadbeater	434	Lecoq	467
Lavar	396	League	434	Lecou	468
Lavat	397	Leak	435	Lecr	469
Lavau	398	Leam	436	Lect	471
Lave	399	Lean	437	Lecture	471
Lavi	411	Lear	438	Led	472
Lavil	412	Leav	439	Lede	473
Lavis	413	Leb	441	Ledo	474
Lavo	414	Lebe	442	Ledr	475
Law	415	Leber	443	Ledy	476
Law, M.	416	Lebi	444	Lee	477
Lawania	416	Lebl	445	Lee	477
Lawe	417	Leblo	446	Lee, G.	478
Lawl	418	Lebo	447	Lee, M.	479
Lawrance	419	Lebor	448	Lee, S.	481
Lawrence, G.	421	Lebou	449	Lee, W.	482
Lawrence, M.	422	Lebr	451	Leec	483

Leed	484	Leho	524	Lemon	556
Leek	485	Lehr	524	Lemonn	557
Leela	485	Lei	525	Lemot	558
Leen	486	Leic	526	Lemoy	559
Lees	487	Leid	527	Lemp	561
Lef	488	Leig	528	Lemu	562
Lefebv	489	Leigh, M.	529	Len	563
Lefer	491	Lein	531	Lend	564
Lefeu	492	Leis	532	Lene	565
Lefev	493	Leit	533	Leng	566
Lefo	494	Lej	534	Lenn	567
Lefr	495	Lejo	535	Lennox	568
Leg	496	Lek	536	Leno	569
Legal	496	Lekh	536	Lenoir	571
Legar	497	Lel	537	Lenor	572
Legat	498	Leland,M	538	Lens	573
Lege	499	Lele	539	Lent	574
Legen	511	Leli	541	Lenz	575
Leger	512	Lell	542	Leo	576
Legg	513	Lelo	543	Leod	577
Legi	514	Lem	544	Leof	578
Legn	515	Lemai	545	Leon	579
Lego	516	Lemais	546	Leonard	581
Legr	517	Lemait	547	Leonc	582
Legras	518	Lemar	548	Leone	583
Legro	519	Lemas	549	Leonh	584
Legu	521	Leme	551	Leoni	585
Leh	522	Lemere	552	Leont	586
Lehm	523	Lemet	553	Leop	587
Lehnery	523	Lemi	554	Leot	588
Lehnus	523	Lemo	555	Leow	589

Lep	591	Leslie, G.	635	Levis	666
Lepai	592	Leslie, M.	636	Levr	667
Lepau	593	Leslie, S.	637	Levy	668
Lepe	594	Less	638	Lew	669
Lepell	595	Lesser	638	Lewe	671
Lepi	596	Lessi	639	Lewin	672
Lepl	597	Lesso	641	Lewis	673
Lepo	598	Lesson	641	Lewis, G.	674
Lepr	599	Lest	642	Lewis, M.	675
Leps	611	Lestr	643	Lewis, S.	676
Lepu	612	Lesu	644	Lewis, W.	677
Leq	613	Let	645	Lewk	678
Ler	614	Letell	646	Lex	679
Lerd	615	Leth	647	Ley	681
Lerm	616	Leti	648	Leybu	682
Lero	617	Leto	649	Leyd	683
Leroux	618	Lett	651	Leyl	684
Leroy	619	Leu	652	Leys	685
Leroy, M.	621	Leul	653	Lez	686
Les	622	Leus	654	Lezo	687
Lesb	623	Lev	655	Lh	688
Lesc	624	Lev	655	Lheu	689
Lesch	625	Levas	656	Lho	691
Lesco	626	Leve	657	Lhu	692
Lescu	627	Lever	658	Li	693
Lesd	628	Lever, M.	659	Lib	694
Lesg	629	Levere	661	Liber	695
Lesl	631	Leves	662	Libo	696
Lesley	632	Levet	663	Libr	697
Lesley, M.	633	Levi	664	Library	697
Leslie	634	Levin	665	Lic	698

Licas	698
Licht	699
Lici	711
Lid	712
Liddo	713
Lide	714
Lido	715
Lie	716
Liebn	717
Liec	718
Lief	719
Lieu	721
Lig	723
Lightf	724
Lign	725
Ligo	726
Ligu	727
Lih	727
Lil	728
Lill	729
Lily	731
Lim	732
Limb	733
Limi	734
Lin	735
Linc	736
Lincoln, G.	737
Lincoln, M.	738
Lincoln, S.	739
Lincoln, W.	741
Lind	742
Linda	742
Linde	743
Linden	744
Lindes	745
Lindf	745
Lindl	746
Lindn	747
Linds	748
Lindsay, M.	749
Lindsel	751
Lindsey	752
Lindsey, M.	753
Lindw	754
Ling	755
Lini	756
Link	756
Linl	757
Linn	758
Lins	759
Lint	761
Linux	761
Linw	762
Lio	763
Lion	763
Lip	764
Lipp	765
Lippm	766
Lips	767
Lir	768
Lis	769
Lisl	771
Liss	772
List	773
Lisz	774
Lit	775
Litch	776
Litte	777
Littl	778
Little	778
Littleb	779
Littlet	781
Littr	782
Liu	783
Liv	784
Live	784
Livermore, M.	785
Livings	786
Livingston, M.	787
Livingstone	788
Liz	789
Ll	791
Llo	792
Lloyd	793
Lly	794
Llyod	794
Lo	795
Lob	796
Loba	796
Lobe	797
Lobk	798
Lobo	799
Loc	811

Local	811	Lokesh	836	Loomba	863
Loch	812	Loknath	836	Lop	864
Lock	813	Lokpur	836	Lopez	864
Locke	814	Loksabha	836	Lor	865
Locker	815	Lol	837	Lord	866
Lockh	816	Lolm	838	Lord, M.	867
Lockw	817	Lom	839	Lore	868
Lockwood	817	Lombard	841	Lorenz	869
Locky	818	Lombardi	842	Lorg	871
Loco	819	Lombe	843	Lori	872
Lod	821	Lombr	844	Loring	873
Lodg	822	Lome	845	Loring, M.	874
Lodha	822	Lomo	846	Lorm	875
Lodhi	822	Lon	847	Lorr	876
Lodi	823	London	847	Lorry	877
Lodo	824	Lone	847	Lort	878
Loe	825	Long	848	Los Angles	879
Loes	826	Long, M.	849	Los	879
Loew	827	Longc	851	Loso	881
Lof	828	Longe	852	Lot	882
Loft	829	Longf	853	Loti	883
Log	831	Longh	854	Lotia	883
Logan	831	Longi	855	Lott	884
Loge	832	Longl	856	Lotz	885
Loghani	832	Longo	856	Lou	886
Loh	833	Longs	857	Loug	887
Lohane	833	Longu	858	Loui	888
Lohia	833	Longus	859	Loun	889
Loi	834	Loni	861	Loup	891
Loisel	835	Lons	862	Lour	892
Lok	836	Loo	863	Lout	893

Louv	894	Luch	936	Lur	967
Louvo	895	Luci	937	Lus	968
Lov	896	Lucin	938	Lush	969
Love	897	Luciu	939	Lusi	971
Lovel	898	Luck	941	Luss	972
Lovell	899	Lucknow	941	Lut	973
Lovell, M.	911	Lucky	941	Luthra	973
Low	912	Lucr	942	Luto	974
Lowe	913	Lucy	943	Lutz	975
Lowell	914	Lud	944	Luv	976
Lowell, G.	915	Ludden	944	Lux	977
Lowell, M.	916	Ludl	945	Luxman	977
Lowell, S.	917	Ludo	946	Luxu	977
Lowi	918	Ludr	947	Luy	978
Lown	919	Ludw	948	Luz	979
Lowr	921	Luf	949	Ly	981
Lowt	922	Lug	951	Lyall	981
Loy	923	Lui	952	Lycu	982
Loy	923	Luis	953	Lyd	983
Loys	924	Luk	954	Lye	984
Loz	925	Lul	955	Lyell	984
Lu	926	Lully	956	Lyl	985
Lubana	926	Lum	957	Lym	986
Lubbo	927	Luml	958	Lyn	987
Lube	928	Lums	959	Lynch	988
Lubi	929	Lun	961	Lynd	988
Luc	931	Lund	962	Lyndgoh	988
Lucan	932	Lung	963	Lynn	989
Lucas	933	Lunt	964	Lyo	991
Lucc	934	Lup	965	Lyon	991
Luce	935	Lupt	966	Lyr	992

Lys	993
Lysi	994
Lyso	995
Lyt	996
Lyttl	997
Lytto	998
Lyv	999

M

Ma	111
Mab	112
Mac	113
Mac	113
Macal	114
Macanlly	114
Macar	115
Macart	116
Macau	117
Macaulitle	117
Macb	118
Macbr	119
Macc	121
Maccal	122
Maccar	123
Macch	124
Macci	125
Maccl	126
Maccli	127
Macclu	128
Macco	129
Maccor	131
Maccr	132
Maccu	133
Macd	134
Macdon	135
Macdonald	135
Macdonn	136
Macdou	137
Macdow	138
Macdowell	138
Macdu	139
Mace	141
Macer	142
Macf	143
Macfi	144
Macg	145
Macgo	146
Macgr	147
Macgu	148
Mach	149
Macho	151
Maci	152
Mack	153
Mackay	153
Macke	154
Macken	155
Mackengil	156
Mackenz	156
Mackenzie, M.	157
Macki	158
Mackn	159
Macl	161
Maclay	162
Macle	163
Maclean	163
Maclel	164
Macleo	165
Maclu	166
Macm	167
Macmillan	167
Macmu	168
Macmullen	168
Macn	169
Maco	171
Macp	172
Macq	173
Macr	174
Macs	175
Macv	176
Macw	177
Mad	178
Madalli	178
Madam	178
Madan	178
Madanjit	178
Madd	179
Maddison	179
Made	181
Madhav	181
Madhavan	181
Madhok	181
Madhu	181
Madhusudan	181
Madhyapradesh	181

Madi	182	Maharaj	214	Mair	228
Madison	182	Maharashtra	214	Mairo	229
Mado	183	Maharishi	214	Mais	231
Madran	183	Mahashweta	214	Mait	232
Madras	183	Mahatma	214	Maiti	232
Mae	184	Mahavir	214	Maitra	232
Mael	185	Mahbub	214	Maity	232
Maes	186	Mahdi	214	Maj	233
Maf	187	Maheep	214	Majid	233
Mag	188	Mahender	214	Majo	234
Magat	189	Mahesh	214	Major	234
Magazine	189	Maheshwar	214	Majumdar	234
Mage	191	Mahila	214	Maka	235
Magen	192	Mahipal	214	Makhan	235
Magg	193	Mahla	214	Makhija	235
Magi	194	Mahm	215	Makkar	235
Magl	195	Mahmood	215	Mal	236
Magn	196	Maho	216	Mala	236
Magni	197	Mahtab	216	Malala	236
Magno	198	Mai	217	Malan	237
Magnu	199	Maidan	217	Malas	238
Mago	211	Maig	218	Malat	239
Magr	212	Mail	219	Malaya	239
Magu	213	Maille	221	Malb	241
Mah	214	Mailly	222	Malc	242
Mahabharta	214	Maim	223	Malco	243
Mahadevan	214	Main	224	Malcolm	243
Mahajan	214	Maine	225	Mald	244
Mahalingam	214	Maini	225	Male	245
Mahanti	214	Maint	226	Males	246
Mahapatra	214	Mainw	227	Malet	247

Malev	248
Malgavakar	248
Malh	249
Malhan	249
Malhotra	249
Mali	251
Malik	251
Mall	252
Mallet	253
Malli	254
Mallick	254
Mallik	254
Mallo	255
Malm	256
Malo	257
Malogonker	248
Malou	258
Malp	259
Malpani	259
Malt	261
Malv	262
Malviya	262
Malwa	262
Malwal	262
Mam	263
Mame	264
Mami	265
Mamoria	265
Mamous	265
Man	266
Manas	267
Manbekar	278
Manc	268
Manchanda	268
Manci	269
Mand	271
Mandal	271
Mandella	271
Mander	272
Mando	272
Mandr	273
Mane	274
Manek	274
Manet	275
Manf	276
Mang	277
Mangal	277
Mangala	277
Mangat	277
Mangla	277
Mani	278
Manickam	278
Manipur	278
Manisha	278
Manjali	278
Manju	278
Mankar	278
Manl	279
Manmohan	279
Mann	281
Mann, M.	282
Manni	283
Manning, M.	284
Manno	285
Manocha	285
Manohar	285
Manoj	285
Manorma	285
Mans	286
Mansf	287
Mansi	288
Manso	289
Mansoor	289
Mansukhani	289
Mant	291
Mantel	292
Manto	293
Manu	294
Manv	295
Manwani	295
Manz	296
Manzoor	296
Mao	296
Map	297
Mar	298
Marai	299
Marak	299
Maran	311
Maratha	311
Marb	312
Marc	313
Marcel	314
March	315

Marche	316
Marchet	317
Marchm	318
Marci	319
Marco	321
Marcu	322
Marcus	322
Marden	322
Mare	323
Maren	334
Mares	325
Maret	326
Marg	327
Margabandhu	327
Marge	328
Margo	329
Margu	331
Mari	332
Maria	332
Marian	333
Marie	333
Marien	334
Marig	335
Maril	336
Marin	337
Marina	337
Marinda	337
Marine	338
Marini	339
Mario	341
Mariot	342
Mariu	343
Marj	344
Mark	345
Markandan	345
Markendey	345
Markl	346
Marl	347
Marli	348
Marlo	349
Marlow	349
Marm	351
Marmon	352
Marn	353
Maro	354
Marot	355
Marou	356
Marq	357
Marr	358
Marri	359
Marriot	359
Marro	361
Marry	362
Mars	363
Marsd	364
Marsh	365
Marsh, M.	366
Marshal	367
Marshall	367
Marshall, G.	368
Marshall, M.	369
Marshm	371
Marsi	372
Marso	373
Marst	374
Mart	375
Martel	376
Marten	377
Marti	378
Martin	379
Martin, G.	381
Martin, M.	382
Martin, S.	383
Martind	384
Martine	385
Martini	386
Marto	387
Marty	388
Maru	389
Maruti	389
Marv	391
Marvin	391
Marwah	391
Marx	392
Mary	393
Mas	394
Masani	394
Masc	395
Mase	396
Mash	397
Masih	396
Maso	398
Mason	398

Mason, G.	399
Mason, M.	411
Mason, S.	412
Masood	412
Masq	413
Mass	414
Masse	415
Massey	416
Massi	417
Massing	418
Masso	419
Masson, M.	421
Massu	422
Mast	423
Master	423
Masu	424
Masud	424
Mat	425
Math	426
Mathar	426
Matharu	426
Mather	427
Mathew	428
Mathews	429
Mathi	431
Matho	432
Mathur	432
Mati	433
Mats	434
Matt	435
Matth	436
Matthew	437
Matthews	438
Matthews, C.	439
Matthews, M.	441
Matthews, S.	442
Matthi	443
Matti	444
Mattoo	444
Matu	445
Maty	446
Mau	447
Mauds	448
Maug	449
Maulana	449
Maun	451
Maup	452
Maur	453
Mauri	454
Maurice	454
Maurice, M.	455
Maurit	456
Mauro	457
Mauru	458
Maurus	458
Maury	459
Maurya	459
Mav	461
Mavi	461
Maw	462
Max	463
Maxi	464
Maxmullar	464
Maxw	465
Maxwell	465
May	466
May, M.	467
Maya	467
Mayer	468
Mayfair	469
Mayh	469
Mayn	471
Mayne	472
Mayo	473
Mayor	474
Mayr	474
Maz	475
Maze	476
Mazhar	476
Mazoor	476
Mazumdar	476
Mazz	477
Mazzon	478
McCarthy	478
McCormic	478
McDonald	478
McGregar	478
McLeod	478
McN	478
Me	479
Meade	481
Meado	482
Mean	483

Meas	484
Meb	485
Mec	486
Meck	487
Med	488
Medi	489
Media	489
Medical	489
Medin	491
Medo	492
Medu	493
Medve	493
Mee	494
Meen	494
Meer	495
Meerut	495
Meg	496
Meger	497
Megh	497
Meghalya	497
Meghna	497
Meh	498
Mehboob	498
Mehdi	498
Mehdiratta	498
Meher	498
Mehra	498
Mehrotra	498
Mehta	498
Mehtab	498
Mehtani	498
Mei	499
Meier	511
Meig	512
Meil	513
Mein	514
Meis	515
Mej	516
Mel	517
Melc	518
Mele	519
Melf	521
Meli	522
Melis	523
Melkote	523
Mell	524
Mellen	525
Melli	526
Mello	527
Melo	528
Melu	529
Melv	531
Melwani	531
Melz	532
Mem	533
Men	534
Menar	535
Menc	536
Mend	537
Mendes	538
Mendh	538
Mendo	539
Mene	541
Menen	542
Menes	543
Meng	544
Meni	545
Menl	546
Menn	547
Menon	547
Mens	548
Ment	549
Menz	551
Mer	552
Merc	553
Mercer	554
Merchant	554
Merci	555
Merco	556
Mercy	557
Mere	558
Meredith	559
Meret	571
Meri	561
Merin	562
Meriv	563
Merl	564
Merli	565
Merm	566
Mero	567
Merr	568
Merrif	569
Merril	571

Merrit	572	Meyr	615	Mill	645
Merry	573	Meys	616	Mille	646
Mers	574	Mez	617	Miller	647
Mert	575	Mi	618	Miller, G.	648
Merv	576	Mic	619	Miller, M.	649
Merz	577	Mich	621	Miller, S.	651
Mes	578	Michael	621	Miller, W.	652
Meshram	578	Michau	622	Millet	653
Mesm	579	Miche	623	Milli	654
Mesn	581	Michi	624	Millin	655
Mesni	582	Micho	625	Millo	656
Mess	583	Mico	626	Mills	657
Messe	584	Mid	627	Milm	658
Messi	585	Middleton	628	Miln	659
Mest	586	Middleton, M.	629	Milo	661
Met	587	Midha	629	Milt	662
Metc	588	Mie	631	Min	663
Mete	589	Mier	632	Minaz	663
Metey	591	Mif	633	Mind	663
Meth	592	Mig	634	Mine	664
Meto	593	Miglani	634	Minhas	664
Metr	594	Mign	635	Mini	665
Mett	595	Migno	636	Minister	665
Metz	596	Mil	637	Mino	666
Meu	597	Milb	638	Mint	667
Meur	598	Milc	639	Minu	668
Meus	599	Mild	641	Mio	669
Mew	611	Mile	642	Mir	671
Mey	612	Miles	643	Mira	671
Meyer, M.	613	Milf	644	Miran	672
Meyn	614	Mili	644	Mirb	673

Mirchandani	673	Modes	691	Molin	722
Mirdha	673	Modi	692	Molini	723
Mire	674	Mody	692	Molis	724
Miri	675	Moe	693	Molit	725
Mirie	676	Moer	694	Moll	726
Miro	676	Mof	695	Mollo	727
Mirz	677	Mog	696	Molo	728
Mirza	677	Moghe	696	Molt	729
Mis	678	Mohammad	697	Moly	731
Mishra	678	Mohan	697	Mom	732
Misra	678	Mohanti	697	Momin	732
Mistri	678	Mohanty	697	Momm	733
Mit	679	Mohapatra	697	Mon	734
Mital	679	Mohinder	697	Monal	735
Mitali	679	Mohit	697	Monas	736
Mitar	679	Mohl	697	Monc	737
Mitchell	681	Mohl	698	Moncl	738
Mitchell, M.	682	Mohr	699	Moncr	739
Mitf	683	Mohsin	699	Mond	741
Mith	684	Mohu	711	Mondal	741
Mithani	684	Moi	712	Mone	742
Mitra	684	Moir	713	Mong	743
Mitt	685	Mois	714	Monga	743
Mittal	685	Moit	715	Mongal	743
Mittar	685	Moitra	715	Mongir	743
Miz	685	Mok	716	Moni	744
Mn	686	Mokashi	716	Monier	744
Mo	687	Mol	717	Monk	745
Moce	688	Mole	718	Monke	745
Mod	689	Moles	719	Monl	746
Modak	689	Moli	721	Monm	747

Monn	748
Monni	749
Mono	751
Monocha	751
Monr	752
Monroe	753
Mons	754
Monso	755
Monst	756
Mont	757
Montag	758
Montague	759
Montai	761
Montal	762
Montale	763
Montan	764
Montano	765
Montar	766
Montau	767
Montb	768
Montbr	769
Montc	771
Monte	772
Monteb	773
Montef	774
Monteg	775
Montel	776
Montem	777
Monter	778
Montes	779
Montess	781
Montessori	781
Montf	782
Montfl	783
Montfo	784
Montg	785
Montgo	786
Montgom	787
Montgomery, M.	788
Month	789
Monti	791
Montig	792
Montl	793
Montlu	794
Montm	795
Montmi	796
Montmo	797
Monto	798
Montp	799
Montr	811
Montri	812
Montro	813
Montv	814
Monu	815
Monz	816
Moo	817
Moody	817
Mool	817
Moon	818
Moor	819
Moore	821
Moore, G.	822
Moore, M.	823
Moore, S.	824
Moore, W.	825
Moorthy	825
Moq	826
Mor	827
Moral	828
Moran	829
Moras	831
Morat	832
Moraz	832
Morc	833
Mord	834
More	835
More, M.	836
Moreau	837
Moreh	838
Morel	839
Morell	841
Morelli	842
Moren	843
Moret	844
Moreti	845
Morf	846
Morg	847
Morgan	848
Morgan, G.	848
Morgan, M.	849
Morge	851
Morgeus	852
Morh	853

Mori	854	Mortaz	832	Moult	927
Morie	855	Morti	888	Moulvi	927
Morig	856	Morto	889	Moun	928
Moril	857	Morton, M.	891	Mour	929
Morin	858	Morv	892	Moure	931
Morini	859	Mory	893	Mous	932
Moris	861	Mos	894	Mouss	933
Morit	862	Mosch	895	Mout	934
Morl	863	Moscho	896	Mov	935
Morle	864	Mose	897	Mow	936
Morlo	865	Mosel	898	Mowli	936
Morn	866	Moser	899	Mox	937
Moro	867	Moses	899	Moy	938
Moron	868	Mosl	912	Moz	939
Moros	869	Moss	913	Mridulla	939
Moroz	871	Mosso	914	Mu	941
Morr	872	Most	915	Muc	942
Morrell	873	Mosto	916	Mud	943
Morri	874	Mot	917	Mudaliar	943
Morris	875	Mote	917	Mudg	944
Morris, G.	876	Moth	918	Mudgal	944
Morris, M.	877	Mother	918	Mudi	945
Morrison	878	Moti	918	Muel	946
Morrison, M.	881	Motl	919	Mueller, M.	947
Morrison, S.	882	Mott	921	Muen	948
Morrison, W.	883	Motte	922	Muf	949
Mors	884	Motz	923	Mufti	949
Morse	885	Mou	924	Mug	951
Morse, G.	885	Mouf	925	Mugals	951
Morse, M.	886	Moul	926	Muh	952
Mort	887	Moulik	926	Muhamed	952

Mui	953
Muir	953
Mujeeb	953
Mukalel	953
Mukerjee	953
Mukesh	953
Mukh	953
Mukhi	953
Mukhia	953
Mukhopadhyay	953
Muktananda	953
Mukund	953
Mul	954
Mulay	954
Muley	954
Mulf	955
Mulg	956
Muli	957
Mulia	958
Mulik	958
Mull	958
Mulli	959
Mullick	959
Mulr	961
Multani	961
Mum	962
Mun	963
Munck	964
Mund	965
Munda	965
Munde	965
Mundra	965
Munf	966
Muni	966
Munjal	966
Munk	966
Muno	967
Munr	968
Muns	969
Munshi	969
Munt	971
Mur	972
Murad	972
Murali	972
Murc	973
Murd	974
Mure	975
Murg	976
Muri	977
Murickan	977
Murli	977
Murngan	977
Murp	978
Murphy	978
Murr	979
Murray	981
Murray, G.	982
Murray, M.	983
Murray, S.	984
Murthi	984
Murthy	984
Murty	984
Mus	985
Musa	985
Muse	986
Musfts	986
Musg	987
Musharraf	987
Mushirul	987
Mushtaq	987
Musp	988
Muss	989
Must	991
Mustafa	991
Mut	992
Muthuswami	992
Mutr	993
Muttalib	993
Muz	994
Muzumdar	994
My	995
Myall	995
Mye	996
Myer	996
Myl	997
Mynmar	997
Myr	998
Myt	999

N

Na	111
Naas	112
Nab	113
Nabar	113

Nabb	114	Naek	142	Naim	157
Nabe	115	Nael	143	Naipaul	157
Nabhi	115	Naer	144	Nair	158
Nabi	116	Naev	145	Nait	159
Nabo	117	Naf	146	Naiv	161
Nac	118	Nag	147	Naj	162
Nach	119	Naga	147	Nak	163
Nachi	121	Nagaland	147	Naki	163
Nachm	122	Nagar	147	Nakra	163
Nacho	123	Nagaraj	147	Nakw	164
Nacht	124	Nagarjuna	147	Nal	165
Nack	125	Nagaswami	147	Naldi	166
Nad	126	Nagendra	147	Naldin	167
Nadal	127	Nageshwar	147	Naldo	168
Nadala	134	Naghar	147	Nale	169
Nadar	128	Nagi	148	Nali	171
Nadas	129	Nagl	149	Nalini	171
Nadast	131	Nagla	149	Nall	172
Nadau	132	Nagli	151	Nals	173
Nadaul	133	Nago	152	Nam	174
Nadda	133	Nagpal	152	Nambiar	174
Nade	134	Nagpur	152	Namboodaripad	174
Nader	135	Nah	153	Namdar	174
Nadi	136	Nahar	153	Nan	175
Nadig	136	Nahl	154	Nana	175
Nadj	137	Nai	155	Nanak	175
Nadkarni	137	Naib	155	Nanavati	175
Nado	138	Naidoo	155	Nanc	176
Nadvi	138	Naidu	155	Nand	176
Nae	139	Naik	155	Nanda	176
Naeg	141	Nail	156	Nandan	176

Nandi	176
Nandy	176
Nane	177
Nang	178
Nangia	178
Nani	179
Nanin	181
Nanini	182
Nanjudappa	182
Nann	183
Nanni	184
Nanno	185
Nannu	186
Nanq	187
Nans	188
Nanso	189
Nant	191
Nanteu	192
Nanti	193
Nao	194
Nap	195
Napier	196
Napier, C.	197
Napier, F.	198
Napier, J.	199
Napier, M.	211
Napier, S.	212
Napier, W.	213
Napio	214
Napl	215
Napo	216
Napoleon	216
Napp	217
Naqvi	217
Nar	218
Narang	218
Narasimha	218
Narayan	218
Narayanamurthy	218
Narbo	219
Narbor	221
Narc	222
Nard	223
Nardin	224
Nare	225
Narendra	225
Nares	226
Nares, M.	227
Naresh	227
Narg	228
Nargis	228
Nargolkar	228
Nari	229
Nariman	229
Narin	231
Narla	231
Narlikar	231
Narn	232
Naro	232
Narp	233
Narr	234
Nars	235
Narst	236
Naru	237
Narula	237
Narv	238
Narvane	238
Narvy	239
Narw	238
Nas	241
Nasaf	242
Nasain	242
Nasal	243
Nasc	244
Nasco	245
Nase	246
Naseem	246
Naser	247
Nash	248
Nash, F.	249
Nash, J.	251
Nash, M.	252
Nash, S.	253
Nasi	254
Nasir	254
Nasm	255
Nasmith	256
Nasmith, M.	257
Nasmyth	258
Nasmyth, M.	259
Naso	261
Nasol	262
Nason	263

Nasr	264
Nass	265
Nassau	266
Nasse	267
Nassi	268
Nast	269
Nat	271
Natali	272
Natar	273
Nath	274
Nathan	274
Nathans	275
Nathu	276
Nati	277
National	277
Nativ	278
Nato	279
Natraja	279
Natrajan	279
Natt	281
Natte	282
Natti	283
Natto	284
Natu	285
Natwar	285
Natz	286
Nau	287
Naub	288
Nauc	289
Naud	291
Naudet	292
Naudi	293
Naudo	294
Naue	295
Nauer	296
Naug	297
Naul	298
Naum	299
Naumann, M.	311
Naun	312
Naus	313
Nauss	314
Nautiyal	314
Nauz	315
Nav	316
Navada	316
Navag	317
Navai	318
Naval	318
Navalani	318
Navar	319
Navarr	321
Navarro	322
Navdeep	322
Nave	323
Naveen	323
Navez	324
Navi	325
Navil	326
Navlekar	326
Navneet	326
Navo	327
Navtej	327
Navy	327
Naw	328
Nawab	328
Nawr	329
Nay	331
Nayak	331
Nayar	331
Nayli	332
Naylo	333
Nayyar	333
Naz	334
Nazar	335
Nazi	335
Nazo	336
Nazz	337
Ne	338
Neal, F.	339
Neal, J.	341
Neal, M.	342
Neal, S.	343
Neal, W.	344
Neale	345
Neale, G.	346
Neale, M.	347
Neale, S.	348
Neander	349
Neander, J.	351
Neander, P.	352
Neap	353
Near	354

Neat	355	Neg	384	Nelson, C.	425
Neate	356	Negi	384	Nelson, F.	426
Neav	357	Negr	385	Nelson, J.	427
Neb	358	Negri	386	Nelson, M.	428
Nebe	359	Negri, G.	387	Nelson, R.	429
Neben	361	Negri, M.	388	Nelson, S.	431
Nebr	362	Negri, S.	389	Nelson, W.	432
Nebu	363	Negri, W.	391	Nem	433
Nec	364	Negrier	392	Nema	433
Neck	365	Negro	393	Nemi	434
Necker	366	Negron	394	Nemn	435
Necker, M.	367	Neh	395	Nemo	436
Neco	368	Nehr	396	Nen	437
Nect	369	Nehru	396	Nene	437
Ned	371	Nei	397	Neno	437
Nee	372	Neil	398	Neo	438
Neeb	373	Neile	399	Neog	438
Need	374	Neill	411	Neogi	438
Needham, M.	375	Neill, J.	412	Nep	439
Neef	376	Neill, P.	413	Nepal	439
Neefe	377	Neils	414	Nepo	441
Neel	378	Neip	415	Nepos	442
Neela	378	Neis	416	Ner	443
NeelaKanta	378	Neit	417	Nere	444
Neelameghan	378	Nek	418	Neri	445
Neele	379	Nel	419	Nerin	446
Neelkamal	379	Nell	421	Nerit	447
Neer	381	Nelli	422	Nerl	448
Neeraj	381	Nello	423	Nero	449
Nees	382	Nels	424	Neroc	451
Nef	383	Nelson	425	Neron	452

Ners	453	Neug	484	Nevins	527
Neru	454	Neuh	485	Nevins, M.	528
Nerv	455	Neuk	486	Nevit	529
Nervet	456	Neul	487	Nevy	531
Nes	457	Neum	488	New	532
Nesb	458	Neuman, G.	491	Newb	533
Nese	459	Neuman, M.	492	Newbe	534
Neshla	459	Neumar	493	Newbu	535
Nesl	461	Neun	494	Newc	536
Nesm	462	Neus	495	Newco	537
Ness	463	Neusi	496	Newcomb, M.	538
Nessel	464	Neut	497	Newcombe	539
Nessi	465	Neuv	498	Newcome	541
Nessm	466	Nev	499	Newd	542
Nesso	467	Neve	511	Newe	543
Nest	468	Neve	511	Newell	544
Net	469	Nevel	512	Newell, G.	545
Netaji	469	Never	513	Newell, M.	546
Netan	469	Nevers	514	Newell, S.	547
Nets	471	Nevers, G.	515	Newh	548
Nett	472	Nevers, M.	516	Newhall	548
Nette	473	Nevers, S.	517	Newl	549
Netter	474	Nevers, W.	518	Newm	551
Nettl	475	Neveu	519	Newman	551
Nettleton, M.	476	Nevi	521	Newman, D.	552
Neu	477	Nevile	521	Newman, J.	553
Neube	478	Nevill	522	Newman, M.	554
Neud	479	Neville	523	Newman, S.	555
Neue	481	Neville, J.	524	Newman, W.	556
Neuf	482	Neville, P.	525	Newn	557
Neufv	483	Nevin	526	Newp	558

News	558
Newt	559
Newton	561
Newton, C.	562
Newton, F.	563
Newton, J.	564
Newton, M.	565
Newton, S.	566
Newton, W.	567
Ney	568
Ney, J.	569
Ney, P.	571
Neyl	572
Neyn	573
Neyr	574
Nez	575
Ng	576
Ni	577
Niazi	577
Nib	578
Nibe	579
Nibo	581
Nic	582
Nican	583
Nicc	584
Niccoli	585
Niccolini	586
Niccolo	587
Nice	588
Nicep	589
Nicer	591
Nicet	592
Nicetas	593
Nich	594
Nichol	595
Nichol, M.	596
Nicholas	597
Nicholas, J.	598
Nicholas, P.	599
Nicholl	611
Nicholl, M.	612
Nicholls	613
Nicholls, G.	614
Nicholls, M.	615
Nichols	616
Nichols, C.	617
Nichols, F.	618
Nichols, J.	619
Nichols, M.	621
Nichols, S.	622
Nichols, W.	623
Nicholson	624
Nicholson, D.	625
Nicholson, J.	626
Nicholson, M.	627
Nicholson, S.	628
Nicholson, W.	629
Nici	631
Nick	632
Nico	633
Nicol	634
Nicolai	635
Nicolai, J.	636
Nicolai, P.	637
Nicolas	638
Nicolau	639
Nicolay	641
Nicole	642
Nicolet	643
Nicoli	644
Nicoll	645
Nicollet	646
Nicolls	647
Nicolls, J.	648
Nicolls, P.	649
Nicolo	651
Nicols	652
Nicolson	653
Nicolson, M.	654
Nicom	655
Nicome	656
Nicon	657
Nicop	658
Nicor	659
Nicos	661
Nicot	662
Nicou	663
Nid	664
Nie	665
Nied	666
Niel	667
Niell	668
Niels	669

Niem	671
Nieme	672
Niemo	673
Niep	674
Nier	675
Niero	676
Niet	677
Nieu	678
Nieul	679
Nieup	681
Nieuw	682
Nif	683
Nig	684
Nigam	684
Niger	685
Niget	686
Nigh	687
Nightengale, M.	688
Nightingale	687
Nigr	689
Nih	691
Nihal	691
Nijhawan	691
Nijjar	691
Nik	692
Nikam	692
Nikhil	692
Niko	693
Nikon	694
Nil	695
Nila	695
Niles	696
Niles, D.	697
Niles, J.	698
Niles, M.	699
Niles, S.	711
Niles, W.	712
Nilima	712
Nilkanta	712
Nim	713
Nimbhkar	713
Nin	714
Nina	714
Ninan	714
Nini	715
Nino	716
Ninu	717
Nio	718
Nip	719
Niq	721
Niraj	721
Niranjan	721
Nirmal	721
Nirupma	721
Nis	722
Nisar	722
Nisb	723
Nisbet, M.	724
Nishan	724
Nishe	724
Nisl	725
Niss	726
Nissan	726
Nisso	727
Nit	728
Nith	729
Nitish	729
Nito	731
Nits	732
Nitt	733
Nitya	733
Niv	734
Nivas	734
Nivedita	734
Niver	735
Nix	736
Niz	737
Nizam	737
Nizami	737
Nj	738
Nm	738
No	739
Noah	739
Noail	741
Noailles, M.	742
Noak	743
Nob	744
Nobi	745
Nobl	746
Noble	747
Noble	747
Noble, D.	748
Noble, J.	749

Noble, M.	751
Noble, S.	752
Noble, W.	753
Nobr	754
Noby	755
Noc	756
Noch	757
Noci	758
Nocr	759
Nod	761
Nodu	762
Noe	763
Noed	764
Noel	765
Noel, D.	766
Noel, J.	767
Noel, M.	768
Noel, S.	769
Nocs	771
Noet	772
Nof	773
Nog	774
Nogaro	775
Noge	776
Nogh	777
Nogu	778
Noh	779
Nohr	781
Noi	782
Noiret	783
Noirot	784
Nok	785
Nol	786
Nolan	787
Nolan, J.	788
Nolan, P.	789
Nold	791
Noli	792
Noll	793
Nollek	794
Nollet	795
Nolli	796
Nolp	797
Nolt	798
Nom	799
Nomu	811
Non	812
Noni	813
Nonn	814
Nonz	815
Noo	816
Noom	817
Noor	818
Noorani	818
Noot	819
Nop	821
Nor	822
Norbert	823
Norbert, M.	824
Norbl	825
Norbu	825
Norby	826
Norc	827
Nord	828
Norden	829
Nordenh	831
Nordens	832
Nordt	833
Nore	834
Norf	835
Norfolk, J.	836
Norfolk, P.	837
Norg	838
Norgay	838
Norgh	839
Nori	841
Norm	842
Norman	842
Norman, M.	843
Normanb	844
Normand	845
Normand, J.	846
Normand, P.	847
Normandy	848
Normann	849
Normant	851
Noro	852
Norr	853
Norris	854
Norris, C.	854
Norris, F.	855
Norris, J.	856
Norris, M.	857

Norris, R.	858	Norway	892	Nouv	934
Norris, S.	859	Norwich, M.	893	Nov	935
Norris, W.	861	Norwo	894	Novar	936
Norry	862	Norwood, M.	895	Nove	937
Nors	863	Norz	896	Novelli	938
North	864	Nos	897	Novello	939
North, G.	865	Nost	898	Nover	941
North, M.	866	Not	899	Noves	942
North, S.	867	Notary	899	Novi	943
Northa	868	Note	911	Novio	944
Northampton	869	Noth	912	Noviu	945
Northampton, M.	871	Notk	913	Now	946
Northb	872	Notr	914	Nowe	947
Northc	873	Nott	915	Nowell, M.	948
Northe	874	Nott, G.	916	Noy	949
Northn	875	Nott, M.	917	Noy	959
Northo	876	Nott, S.	918	Noyer	951
Northr	877	Notti	919	Noyes	952
Northu	878	Nottingham, M.	921	Noyes, C.	953
Northw	879	Nottn	922	Noyes, F.	954
Northwo	881	Notto	923	Noyes, J.	955
Norto	882	Nou	924	Noyes, M.	956
Norton, C.	883	Noue	925	Noyes, R.	957
Norton, F.	884	Nouet	926	Noyes, S.	958
Norton, J.	885	Noug	927	Noyes, W.	959
Norton, M.	886	Nouh	928	Noz	961
Norton, R.	887	Nouj	928	Nu	962
Norton, S.	888	Noul	929	Nuce	963
Norton, W.	889	Nour	931	Nuci	964
Norv	891	Nourr	932	Nug	965
Norw	892	Nours	933	Nugent	966

Nugent, J.	967
Nugent, S.	968
Nuh	968
Nul	969
Num	971
Nun	972
Nunu	973
Nur	974
Nurane	974
Nurul	974
Nus	975
Nusali	975
Nut	976
Nutt, J.	977
Nutt, P.	978
Nutta	979
Nuttall, M.	981
Nutter	982
Nutter, G.	983
Nutter, M.	984
Nutter, S.	985
Nutting	986
Nutting, G.	987
Nutting, M.	988
Nuv	989
Nuy	991
Nuz	992
Ny	993
Nyak	994
Nye	994
Nyk	995
Nym	996
Nyo	997
Nys	998
Nyt	999
Nyun	999

O

Oa	11
Oak	11
Oates	11
Ob	12
Oberoi	12
Obr	13
Obs	14
Oc	15
Och	16
OCLC	16
Oco	17
Oconn	18
Ocor	19
Oct	21
Od	22
Ode	23
Oden	23
Odi	24
Odisha	24
Odo	25
Odon	26
Odr	27
Oe	28
Oer	29
Of	31
Off	32
Office	32
Ofl	33
Og	34
Ogl	35
Ogle	35
Ogr	35
Oh	36
Ohala	36
Ohdedar	36
Ohe	37
Ohm	38
Ohri	38
Oi	39
Ojha	39
Ok	41
Ol	42
Olb	43
Old	44
Oldenberg	44
Oldhan	44
Ole	45
Olf	45
Oli	46
Olip	47
Oliv	48
Oliver	48
Olivi	49
Olm	51
Olo	52
Olson	52

Oly	53
Om	54
Oman	54
Omar	54
Ome	55
Omkar	55
Omo	56
Omparkash	56
Omu	57
On	58
Onkar	58
Ons	59
Oomen	59
Op	61
Opp	62
Or	63
Orb	64
Orbit	64
Ord	65
Ore	66
Orf	67
Org	68
Ori	69
Oriental	69
Orissa	69
Orl	71
Orlo	72
Orm	73
Orn	74
Orr	75
Ors	76
Ort	77
Orto	78
Orv	79
Os	81
Osama	81
Osborn	81
Osg	82
Osgood	82
Osho	82
Osm	83
Osman	83
Osnran	83
Oss	84
Ost	85
Osw	86
Oswal	86
Ot	87
Ota	87
Oti	88
Ott	89
Ottawa	89
Ottl	91
Otw	92
Ou	93
Ous	94
Ouv	95
Ov	96
Ow	97
Owaisi	97
Owen	97
Ox	98
Oxford	98
Oxy	99
Oye	99
Oz	99
Oza	99

P

Pa	111
Paac	112
Paacu	113
Pabla	113
Pacc	114
Pace	115
Pacey	115
Pach	116
Pachauri	116
Pachori	116
Paci	117
Pacin	118
Pack	119
Packard	119
Paco	121
Pacu	122
Pad	123
Padaki	123
Padam	123
Padda	123
Padey	123
Padganokar	123
Padhi	123
Padhy	123
Padia	123

Name	Number
Padma	123
Padmanabhan	123
Padmini	123
Pado	124
Padu	125
Padukone	125
Padwel	125
Pae	126
Paele	126
Paez	127
Pag	128
Pagani	129
Pagano	131
Pagare	131
Page	132
Page, M.	133
Pagen	134
Paget	135
Pagi	136
Pagit	137
Pagl	138
Pagn	139
Pah	141
Pahariya	141
Pahuja	141
Pahwa	141
Pai	142
Pail	143
Pain	144
Paine, G.	145
Paine, M.	146
Paine, S.	147
Paint	148
Pais	149
Paivi	149
Paj	151
Pak	152
Paken	152
Pakistan	152
Pal	153
Palad	153
Palai	154
Palanithural	154
Palat	154
Palaz	155
Pale	156
Palekar	156
Pales	157
Paley	158
Palf	159
Palg	161
Pali	162
Palis	163
Palit	163
Paliwal	163
Palkhiwala	163
Pall	164
Pallav	165
Palle	166
Palli	167
Pallis	168
Pallu	169
Pallvi	169
Palm	171
Palme	172
Palmer	173
Palmer, G.	174
Palmer, M.	175
Palmer, S.	176
Palmer, W.	177
Palmers	178
Palmes	178
Palmi	179
Palo	181
Pals	182
Palt	183
Palu	184
Palvia	184
Palwinder	184
Pam	185
Pamph	186
Pan	187
Panagariya	187
Panar	187
Panc	188
Panchal	188
Panchan	188
Panchmukhi	188
Panchpakesa	188
Pand	189
Panda	189
Pande	189
Pandey	189

Pandhy	189	Papanek	213	Parf	229
Pandian	189	Pape	214	Pargat	229
Pandikar	189	Papi	215	Pari	231
Pandit	189	Papil	216	Paride	231
Panduranga	189	Papin	217	Parihar	231
Pandya	189	Papo	218	Parikh	231
Pane	191	Papola	218	Paris	232
Panes	191	Paq	219	Parish	233
Pani	192	Par	221	Parisi	234
Panickar	192	Parabhakar	895	Park	235
Panigarhi	192	Parad	222	Park, M.	236
Panija	193	Parakal	222	Parkash	236
Panikar	193	Paraksh	222	Parke	237
Paniz	193	Param	222	Parker	238
Panjab	193	Paramanand	222	Parker, F.	239
Pankas	193	Paramjit	222	Parker, J.	241
Pann	194	Paran	223	Parker, M.	242
Panna	194	Paranjape	223	Parker, S.	243
Panner	194	Paras	223	Parker, W.	244
Pannikar	194	Parasher	223	Parkes	245
Pano	195	Parasnis	223	Parkh	246
Panorama	195	Parasuram	223	Parki	247
Pans	196	Parav	224	Parkinson, M.	248
Pant	197	Parc	225	Parkman	249
Panthare	197	Pard	226	Parkman, M.	251
Panto	198	Pardav	226	Parks	252
Panwar	198	Pare	227	Parm	253
Panz	199	Pareek	227	Parmar	253
Pao	211	Parekh	227	Parment	254
Paolo	212	Parekh	237	Parmi	255
Pap	213	Paren	228	Parmioo	255

Parmod	255
Parn	256
Paro	257
Parr	258
Parr, M.	259
Parri	261
Parro	262
Parrot	263
Parry	264
Parry, M.	265
Pars	266
Parser	266
Parsons	267
Parsons, G.	268
Parsons, M.	269
Parsons, S.	271
Parsons, W.	272
Part	273
Partap	273
Parthasarthi	273
Parto	274
Partr	275
Parulekar	275
Paruthi	275
Parv	276
Parveen	276
Parvez	276
Parvinder	276
Parwal	276
Parwati	276
Pas	277
Pasc	278
Pasch	279
Pasco	281
Pasha	281
Pashura	281
Pasi	282
Paso	283
Pasq	284
Pasricha	284
Pass	285
Passar	286
Passe	287
Passi	288
Passo	289
Past	291
Pasto	292
Pastor	293
Paswan	293
Pat	294
Patanik	294
Patanjali	294
Patankar	294
Pate	295
Patekar	295
Patel	295
Paters	296
Paterson, M.	297
Pathak	297
Pathan	297
Pathania	297
Pathar	297
Pathe	297
Pathy	297
Pati	298
Patiala	298
Patil	298
Patis	299
Patki	299
Patm	311
Patna	311
Patni	311
Pato	312
Patodia	312
Patou	313
Patr	314
Patra	314
Patro	314
Patt	315
Pattabhiram	315
Pattanaik	315
Patten	316
Patterson	317
Patterson, M.	318
Pattes	319
Patti	321
Patto	322
Patwardhan	322
Patwari	322
Pau	323
Paul	324
Pauld	325
Paule	326

Pauli	327	Peace	355	Pell	385
Paulin	328	Peaco	356	Pelle	386
Paull	329	Peak	357	Peller	387
Paulm	331	Peal	358	Pellet	388
Pauls	332	Pear	359	Pellew	389
Paulu	333	Pearl	359	Pelli	391
Paus	334	Pears	361	Pello	392
Pause	334	Pearson	362	Pelt	393
Paut	335	Pearson, M.	362	Pemb	394
Pauw	336	Peas	363	Pemberton, M.	395
Pav	337	Pec	364	Pembr	396
Pavi	338	Pecc	365	Pembs	394
Pavo	339	Peck	366	Pen	397
Pawan	339	Peck, M.	367	Pendl	398
Pawar	339	Peckh	368	Pendse	398
Pawte	339	Peco	369	Penh	399
Pax	341	Ped	371	Peni	411
Paxt	342	Pedro	372	Penn	412
Pay	343	Pee	373	Pennel	413
Payer	344	Peel	374	Penni	414
Paymaster	344	Peer	375	Penno	415
Payn	345	Peg	376	Penny	416
Payne	346	Peggy	376	Penr	417
Pays	347	Pei	377	Pens	418
Paz	348	Peirc	378	Pent	419
Pe	349	Peirs	379	Pentz	419
Peabody	351	Pek	379	Pep	421
Peabody, G.	352	Pel	381	Pepi	422
Peabody, M.	353	Pelet	382	Pepo	423
Peabody, S.	354	Pelh	383	Pepp	424
Peac	355	Peli	384	Pepsi	424

Pepy	425
Per	426
Perau	427
Perc	428
Perci	429
Percival	429
Percy	431
Percy, M.	432
Perd	433
Pere	434
Pereg	435
Perei	436
Perel	437
Perera	437
Perez	438
Perg	439
Peri	441
Perier	442
Perig	443
Perigo	444
Perin	445
Peris	446
Perk	447
Perkins	448
Perkins, J.	449
Perkins, P.	451
Perkinson	451
Pern	452
Pero	453
Perr	454
Perre	455
Perri	456
Perrier	457
Perrin	458
Perro	459
Perrot	461
Perry	462
Perry, G.	463
Perry, M.	464
Perry, S.	465
Pers	466
Perso	467
Pert	468
Perti	469
Peru	471
Perumel	471
Pes	472
Pesc	473
Pese	474
Peshawaria	474
Pess	475
Pest	476
Pestonjee	476
Pet	477
Peter	478
Peterb	479
Peters	481
Peters, J.	482
Peters, P.	483
Petersen	484
Peterson	485
Peth	486
Peti	487
Petis	488
Petit	489
Petito	491
Peto	492
Petr	493
Petrei	494
Petri	495
Petrin	496
Petro	497
Petru	498
Pett	499
Petti	511
Petty	512
Petz	513
Peu	514
Pey	515
Peyro	516
Peys	517
Peyst	518
Peyt	519
Pez	521
Pezr	522
Pf	523
Pfe	524
Pfei	525
Pfeiffer	526
Pfeiffer, M.	527
Pfen	528
Pfi	529
Pfl	531

Ph	532	Phillips, J.	561	Piccio	589
Phad	532	Phillips, M	562	Picco	591
Phadke	532	Phillips, S.	563	Pich	592
Phadnis	532	Phillips, W.	564	Picho	593
Phal	533	Philo	565	Pichumani	593
Phale	534	Philoc	566	Pick	594
Phalke	534	Philom	567	Picker	595
Phan	535	Philos	568	Pickering, M.	596
Phansalkar	535	Philox	569	Picket	597
Phar	536	Philp	571	Pico	598
Phe	537	Phin	572	Picou	599
Phel	538	Phip	573	Pict	611
Phelps, J.	539	Pho	574	Pid	612
Phelps, P.	541	Phogat	574	Pie	613
Pher	542	Phor	575	Pien	614
Phi	543	Phr	576	Pier	615
Phil	544	Phry	577	Pierce, G.	616
Philb	545	Phvkan	577	Pierce, M.	617
Phile	546	Phy	578	Pierce, S.	618
Phili	547	Pi	579	Pierl	619
Philid	548	Pia	579	Pierp	621
Philip	549	Pian	581	Pierr	622
Philipp	551	Piar	581	Pierres	623
Philippi	552	Piat	582	Piers	624
Philippu	553	Piatt	583	Piet	625
Philips	554	Piaz	584	Pietro	626
Philips, M.	555	Pic	585	Pif	627
Phill	556	Picar	586	Pig	628
Phillip	557	Picard	586	Pige	629
Phillips	558	Picc	587	Pigg	631
Phillips, F.	559	Piccin	588	Pign	632

Pigo	633
Pih	634
Pik	635
Pike	635
Pike, M.	636
Pil	637
Piles	638
Pilk	639
Pill	641
Pillai	641
Pillo	642
Pilo	643
Pim	644
Pimpley	644
Pin	645
Pinar	646
Pinc	647
Pinch	647
Pind	648
Pine	649
Pinel	651
Pinet	652
Ping	653
Pingle	653
Pinh	654
Pink	655
Pinn	656
Pino	657
Pins	658
Pint	659
Pinto	659
Pinz	661
Pio	662
Pioz	663
Pip	666
Piper	667
Piq	668
Pir	667
Piramal	667
Pirazads	667
Pirazizs	667
Piri	668
Pirk	669
Piro	671
Piron	672
Pis	673
Pisani	674
Pisano	675
Pisc	676
Pise	677
Piso	678
Pist	679
Pit	681
Pitambar	681
Pitc	682
Pith	683
Pithani	683
Piti	684
Pitm	685
Pitman	685
Pitr	686
Pits	687
Pitt	688
Pitti	689
Pitto	691
Pitts	692
Piu	693
Pix	694
Piz	695
Pl	696
Plac	697
Placi	698
Plan	699
Planchet	711
Plane	712
Planner	712
Plant	713
Planti	714
Plas	715
Plat	716
Platn	717
Plato	718
Platt	719
Plau	721
Play	722
Playfo	723
Ple	724
Plen	725
Ples	726
Pley	727
Pli	728
Plmer	728
Plo	729

Plott	729	Polak	762	Pon	792
Plou	731	Poland	762	Poncel	793
Plow	732	Pole	763	Poncet	794
Plu	733	Polem	764	Ponch	795
Plum	734	Polen	765	Pond	796
Plumm	735	Poli	766	Pondichery	796
Plump	736	Police	766	Pong	796
Plun	737	Policy	766	Poni	797
Pluy	738	Polier	767	Pons	798
Po	739	Polig	768	Ponso	799
Poco	741	Polit	769	Pont	811
Pod	742	Poll	771	Pontb	812
Poddar	742	Pollard, M.	772	Ponte	813
Poe	743	Polle	773	Pontec	814
Poel	744	Polli	774	Pontev	815
Poer	745	Pollio	775	Ponti	816
Pog	746	Pollo	776	Pontm	817
Poh	747	Pollock	776	Ponto	818
Pohl	748	Pollock, M.	777	Ponz	819
Poi	749	Polo	778	Poo	821
Poin	751	Polt	779	Poole	822
Poins	752	Poly	781	Poonam	822
Poir	753	Polyc	782	Poone	822
Pois	754	Polym	783	Poor	823
Poisso	755	Pom	784	Poort	824
Poit	756	Pome	785	Pop	825
Poiti	757	Pomf	786	Pope	825
Poix	758	Pomm	787	Pope, M.	826
Poj	759	Pomp	788	Poph	827
Pok	761	Pompi	789	Pophalie	827
Pol	762	Pompo	791	Popi	828

Popley	828	Pot	859	Powers	888
Popo	829	Potdar	859	Pown	889
Popp	831	Pote	861	Poy	891
Popular	831	Poth	862	Poyn	892
Por	832	Poti	863	Poz	893
Porc	833	Poto	864	Pozzo	894
Porci	834	Pott	865	Pr	895
Pord	835	Potter	866	Prabha	895
Pori	836	Potter	866	Prabhakaran	895
Porp	837	Potter, G.	867	Prabhu	895
Porr	838	Potter, M.	868	Prachand	895
Port	839	Potter, S.	869	Prad	896
Portaf	841	Potti	871	Pradeep	896
Portal	842	Pou	872	Pradhan	896
Porte	843	Poudyal	872	Pradhi	896
Porter	844	Poui	873	Prae	897
Porter, F.	845	Poul	874	Praet	898
Porter, J.	846	Poull	875	Prag	898
Porter, M.	847	Poulose	875	Prahalad	898
Porter, S.	848	Poult	876	Prajapal	898
Porter, W.	849	Pour	877	Prajya	898
Porth	851	Pous	878	Prakash	898
Porti	852	Pout	879	Pramod	898
Portm	853	Pow	881	Pran	899
Porwel	853	Powar	881	Pranab	899
Porz	854	Powell	882	Pras	911
Pos	855	Powell, F.	883	Prasad	911
Poss	856	Powell, J.	884	Prasher	911
Post	857	Powell, M.	885	Prat	912
Postel	857	Powell, S.	886	Pratap	912
Postl	858	Power	887	Prath	912

Pratiba	912
Pratima	912
Pratt	913
Pratt, F.	914
Pratt, J.	915
Pratt, M.	916
Pratt, S.	917
Prau	918
Praveen	918
Prax	919
Pray	921
Pre	922
Prec	923
Preetam	923
Prei	924
Prem	925
Premi	925
Pren	926
Prens	926
Prent	927
Prer	927
Pres	928
Prescott	929
Prescott, G.	931
Prescott, M.	932
Prescott, S.	933
President	933
Presl	934
Press	935
Prest	936
Preston	937
Preston, G.	938
Preston, M.	939
Preston, S.	941
Preston, W.	942
Preu	943
Prev	944
Pri	945
Price	945
Price, M.	946
Prich	947
Prie	948
Pries	949
Prieu	951
Prilokar	951
Prim	952
Prime	953
Prin	954
Prince, G.	955
Prince, M.	956
Prince, S.	957
Prio	958
Pris	959
Prit	961
Pritam	961
Prithipal	961
Priya	961
Pro	962
Proc	963
Proct	964
Prof	964
Prohit	964
Prom	965
Pros	966
Prot	967
Prou	968
Prov	969
Pru	971
Prun	972
Pruthi	972
Pry	973
Pryag	973
Ps	974
Pt	975
Pu	976
Pubby	976
Public	976
Puc	977
Pug	978
Pugh	978
Pugwash	978
Pui	979
Pujjari	979
Pul	981
Pull	982
Pulparampil	982
Pult	983
Pun	984
Punam	984
Punekar	984
Pungaliya	984
Punia	984
Punita	984

Punja	984
Punjab	984
Punnoor	984
Pur	985
Puran	985
Puranik	985
Puri	985
Purkayastha	985
Purkit	985
Purohit	985
Purs	986
Purushotam	986
Pus	987
Pusa	987
Pushker	987
Pushp	987
Pushpenler	987
Puskar	987
Pustak	987
Put	988
Putin	988
Putnam	989
Putnam, G.	991
Putnam, M.	992
Putnam, S.	993
Putta	993
Puy	994
Py	995
Pyal	995
Pyarelal	995
Pye	995
Pyl	996
Pylee	996
Pyn	997
Pyr	998
Pyt	999

Q

Qadiri	1
Qaisar	1
Qamar	1
Qamaruddin	1
Qanungo	1
Qarni	1
Qasim	1
Qazi	1
Qua	1
Quat	2
Quayyum	2
Quddus	2
Que	3
Quebec	3
Queen	3
queens	3
Quer	4
Ques	5
Quezon	5
Qui	6
Quin	7
Quincy	7
Quir	8
Quito	8
Quo	9
Quora	9
Quraishi	9
Qureshi	9
Quyamuddin	9

R

Ra	111
Rab	112
Rabau	113
Rabba	112
Rabbani	113
Rabe	114
Raben	115
Rabi	116
Rabinder	116
Rabsa	116
Rabu	117
Rac	118
Rach	119
Rachhpal	119
Raci	121
Racine	121
Rack	122
Raco	123
Rad	124
Radc	125
Rade	126
Radem	127
Radet	128
Radha	128
Radhakrishna	128
Radhaswami	128

Radhe	128
Radhika	128
Radi	129
Rado	131
Radu	132
Radz	133
Rae	134
Rae	134
Raen	135
Raf	136
Raffen	137
Raffl	138
Rafiq	138
Rafn	139
Rag	141
Ragani	141
Ragg	142
Raghav	142
Raghu	142
Raghubir	142
Raghunath	142
Ragl	143
Rago	144
Ragu	145
Ragus	146
Rah	147
Raha	147
Raheja	147
Rahi	147
Rahim	147
Rahman	147
Rahmat	147
Rahn	148
Rahul	148
Rai	149
Raik	151
Raikhy	151
Rail	152
Raim	153
Rain	154
Raina	154
Raine	155
Rainey	156
Raini	157
Raino	158
Rainv	159
Rais	159
Raisina	159
Rait	161
Rait	161
Raizada	161
Raj	161
Raja	161
Rajagopal	161
Rajagopalachari	161
Rajagopalan	161
Rajaiah	161
Rajajee	161
Rajaji	161
Rajalakshmi	161
Rajaman	161
Rajamanickam	161
Rajan	161
Rajap	161
Rajapurohit	161
Rajaram	161
Rajaraman	161
Rajashekhar	161
Rajasthan	161
Rajbans	161
Raje	161
Rajeev	161
Rajendra	161
Rajesh	161
Rajeshwar	161
Rajgopal	161
Rajguru	161
Rajhans	161
Rajinder	161
Rajiv	161
Rajna	161
Rajneesh	161
Rajora	161
Rajpal	161
Rajpur	161
Rajput	161
Rajshekhar	161
Raju	161
Rajvir	161
Rajya	161
Rajyalakshmi	161
Rak	162
Rakes	162

Rakesh	162
Rakshit	162
Ral	163
Ralf	163
Ralhan	163
Ralin	116
Rals	164
Ram	165
Ramachandra	166
Ramacharka	166
Ramacharya	166
Ramadevi	166
Ramaiah	166
Ramakant	166
Ramakrishan	166
Ramakrishan	166
Ramakrishnan	166
Ramamurthi	166
Raman	166
Ramana	166
Ramanatha	166
Ramanathan	166
Ramani	166
Ramanujam	166
Ramasamy	166
Ramaswami	166
Ramayya	166
Ramaz	166
Ramb	167
Rambu	168
Ramd	169
Ramdas	169
Rame	171
Ramel	172
Ramesh	172
Rami	173
Ramjee	173
Ramjilal	173
Ramm	174
Ramo	175
Ramou	176
Ramp	177
Rampal	177
Rams	178
Ramsay, J.	179
Ramsay, P.	181
Ramsd	182
Ramse	183
Ramsey	183
Ramu	184
Ran	185
Rana	185
Ranab	185
Ranade	185
Ranadive	185
Ranbir	185
Rand	186
Rand, M.	187
Randall	188
Randall, M.	189
Rande	191
Randhawa	191
Randhir	191
Rando	192
Randolph, G.	193
Randolph, M.	194
Randon	195
Rane	195
Rang	196
Rangacharya	196
Ranganath	196
Ranganathan	196
Rangaraj	196
Rangarajan	196
Rangaswami	196
Rangila	196
Rangoonwala	196
Rangra	196
Rangwala	196
Rani	197
Ranina	197
Ranjan	197
Rank	198
Ranken	199
Ranki	211
Rans	212
Rant	213
Ranz	214
Rao	215
Rap	216
Raph	217
Rapi	218
Rapo	219

Rapp	221	Rau	239	Ray, M.	264
Rapson	221	Rauch	241	Rayall	263
Ras	222	Rauco	242	Rayan	263
Rasch	223	Raud	243	Rayb	265
Rase	224	Rauf	244	Raychaudhuri	265
Rasgotra	224	Raul	245	Raye	266
Rashed	224	Raum	246	Raym	267
Rashtriya	224	Raun	246	Raymond	268
Rask	225	Raunot	246	Raymond, G.	269
Rasool	225	Raup	247	Raymond, M.	271
Rasp	226	Raus	248	Raymond, S.	272
Raspo	227	Raut	249	Raymond, W.	273
Rass	228	Raut	249	Rayn	274
Rast	229	Rauz	251	Rayne	275
Rasto	231	Rav	252	Rayno	276
Rastogi	231	Raveena	252	Rayo	277
Rat	232	Ravel	252	Raz	278
Ratc	233	Raven	253	Raza	278
Rath	234	Ravens	254	Razoon	279
Rathi	234	Raves	255	Re	281
Ratho	234	Ravi	256	Rea	281
Rathore	234	Ravinder	256	Read	282
Raths	235	Raw	257	Read, H.	283
Rati	236	Rawal	257	Read, M.	284
Ratna	236	Rawat	257	Reade	285
Ratnakar	236	Rawilnson	257	Reade, M.	286
Ratnam	236	Rawl	258	Reading	287
Ratt	237	Rawlin	259	Reag	287
Ratta	237	Rawlinson	261	Real	288
Rattan	232	Raws	262	Reb	289
Ratz	238	Ray	263	Rebell	291

Rebo	292	Reev	331	Reif	361
Rebs	293	Reeve	331	Reil	362
Rec	294	Reeves	332	Reim	363
Recco	295	Reg	333	Rein	364
Rech	296	Regg	334	Reine	365
Rechen	297	Regi	335	Reinec	366
Reck	298	Regio	336	Reiner	367
Recl	299	Regional	336	Reinh	368
Reco	311	Regis	337	Reinhard	369
Red	312	Regmi	337	Reinhart	371
Redd	313	Regn	338	Reinho	372
Reddi	313	Regnau	339	Reinm	373
Reddy	313	Regne	341	Reins	374
Rede	314	Regni	342	Reis	375
Redf	315	Rego	343	Reiset	376
Redg	316	Regu	344	Reisi	377
Redi	317	Reh	345	Reiss	378
Redm	318	Rehani	345	Reit	379
Redmi	318	Reht	346	Rej	381
Redo	319	Rei	347	Rel	382
Redp	321	Reicha	348	Reli	382
Ree	322	Reiche	349	Rell	383
Reed	323	Reichen	351	Rem	384
Reed	323	Reichm	352	Remb	385
Reed, G.	324	Reid	353	Reme	386
Reed, M.	325	Reid, D.	354	Remi	387
Reed, S.	326	Reid, F.	355	Remin	388
Reed, W.	327	Reid, J.	356	Remo	389
Reejhsinghani	327	Reid, M.	357	Remu	391
Rees	328	Reid, S.	358	Remy	392
Reese	329	Reid, W.	359	Ren	393

Renar	394	Ret	437	Rhet	472
Renau	395	Reth	438	Rhi	473
Renaul	396	Rett	439	Rhine	473
Rend	397	Retz	441	Rho	474
Rendu	398	Reu	442	Rhod	475
Rene	399	Reul	443	Rhodes	476
Renes	411	Reum	444	Rhodes, M.	477
Reng	412	Reus	445	Rhodo	478
Reni	413	Reuss	446	Rhou	479
Renn	414	Reut	447	Ri	481
Rennev	415	Reuv	448	Rib	482
Renni	416	Rev	449	Ribb	483
Renny	417	Revell	451	Ribe	484
Reno	418	Rever	452	Riber	484
Renou	419	Reves	453	Ribes	485
Rens	421	Revi	454	Ribo	486
Rent	422	Rex	455	Ric	487
Renu	423	Rey	456	Ricardo	488
Renv	424	Reyb	457	Ricc	489
Rep	425	Reym	458	Ricci	491
Rept	426	Reyn	459	Ricciar	492
Repu	426	Reyni	461	Riccio	493
Req	427	Reyno	462	Ricco	494
Rer	428	Reynolds, G.	463	Rice	495
Res	429	Reynolds, M.	464	Rice, G.	496
Resch	431	Reynolds, S.	465	Rice, M.	497
Rese	432	Reynolds, W.	466	Rich	498
Resen	433	Rez	467	Rich, M.	499
Resn	434	Rh	468	Richard	511
Ress	435	Rhe	469	Richard, G.	512
Rest	436	Rhen	471	Richard, M	513

Richards	514
Richards, F.	515
Richards, J.	516
Richards, M.	517
Richards, S.	518
Richards, W.	519
Richardson	521
Richardson, D.	522
Richardson, J.	523
Richardson, M.	524
Richardson, S.	525
Richardson, W.	526
Riche	527
Richel	528
Richer	529
Richi	531
Richm	532
Richmond, M.	533
Richt	534
Richter	535
Richter, M.	536
Richter, S.	537
Rici	538
Rick	539
Rico	541
Rid	542
Riddel	543
Riddle	543
Ride	544
Ridl	545
Ridley, M.	546
Rido	547
Rie	171
Rie	548
Ried	549
Riedes	551
Riedi	552
Rief	553
Rieg	554
Rieh	555
Riem	556
Rien	557
Riep	558
Ries	559
Riese	561
Riesn	562
Riet	563
Rieu	564
Rig	565
Rigaul	566
Rigb	567
Rige	568
Rigg	569
Righ	571
Rign	572
Rikhye	572
Ril	573
Rill	574
Rim	575
Rimi	576
Rimm	577
Rin	578
Rinc	579
Ring	581
Ringo	582
Rint	583
Rinu	584
Rio	585
Rios	586
Riou	587
Rip	588
Ripley	589
Ripley, H.	591
Ripley, R.	592
Ripp	593
Ripudaman	593
Riq	594
Ris	595
Rishi	595
Riss	596
Rist	597
Rit	598
Ritchie, G.	599
Ritchie, M.	611
Rits	612
Ritt	613
Ritter	614
Ritter, M.	615
Riv	616
Rivan	617
Rivar	618
Rivau	619
Rive	621

Rivers	622	Robin	655	Rodew	689
Rives	623	Robine	656	Rodg	691
Rivet	624	Robins	657	Rodi	692
Rivi	625	Robinson	658	Rodm	693
Rivo	626	Robinson, D.	659	Rodn	694
Riz	627	Robinson, G.	661	Rodo	695
Rizvi	627	Robinson, J.	662	Rodr	696
Ro	628	Robinson, M.	663	Rodw	697
Robar	629	Robinson, S.	664	Roe	698
Robb	631	Robinson, T.	665	Roe, M.	699
Robbins	632	Robinson, W.	666	Roeb	711
Robbins, F.	633	Robs	667	Roed	712
Robbins, J.	634	Roby	668	Roeh	713
Robbins, M.	635	Roc	669	Roel	714
Robbins, S.	636	Rocc	671	Roem	715
Robbins, W.	637	Roch	672	Roep	716
Robe	638	Roche	673	Roer	717
Robert	639	Rochef	674	Roes	718
Robert, G.	641	Rochem	675	Roet	719
Robert, M.	642	Roches	676	Rog	721
Roberts	643	Rochet	677	Roger	722
Roberts, F.	644	Rochf	678	Roger, M.	723
Roberts, J.	645	Rochm	679	Rogers	724
Roberts, M.	646	Rocho	681	Rogers, D.	725
Roberts, S.	647	Rock	682	Rogers, G.	726
Roberts, W.	648	Rocki	683	Rogers, J.	727
Robertson	649	Rockw	684	Rogers, M.	728
Robertson, J.	651	Rod	685	Rogers, S.	729
Robertson, S.	652	Rodd	686	Rogers, W.	731
Robes	653	Rode	687	Roget	732
Robi	654	Roder	688	Rogg	733

Rogi	734
Rogn	735
Rogu	736
Roh	737
Rohilla	737
Rohini	737
Rohit	737
Rohl	738
Rohr	739
Roi	741
Rok	742
Roko	743
Rol	744
Role	745
Rolf	746
Rolfe, M.	747
Roli	748
Roll	749
Rolles	751
Rollett	752
Rolli	753
Rollin	754
Rollo	755
Rolls	755
Rom	756
Romai	757
Roman	758
Romano	759
Romanu	761
Romb	762
Rome	763
Romey	764
Romi	765
Romm	766
Romu	767
Ron	768
Ronc	769
Rond	771
Rone	772
Rong	773
Rons	774
Ronz	775
Roo	776
Rook	777
Roonwal	777
Roop	778
Roor	779
Roos	781
Root	782
Root, M.	783
Rop	784
Ropes	785
Roq	786
Ror	787
Ros	788
Rosa	788
Rosar	789
Rosc	791
Rosco	792
Roscoe, G.	793
Roscoe, M.	794
Rose	795
Rose, G.	796
Rose, M.	797
Roseb	798
Rosec	799
Rosel	811
Rosem	812
Rosen	813
Rosenk	814
Rosenn	815
Rosenw	816
Roset	817
Rosew	818
Roshan	819
Rosi	819
Rosin	821
Rosn	822
Ross	823
Ross, G.	824
Ross, M.	825
Ross, S.	826
Ross, W.	827
Rossel	828
Rosset	829
Rossi	831
Rossi, G.	832
Rossi, M.	833
Rossig	834
Rossin	835
Rossl	836
Rossm	837
Rosso	838

Rost	839	Rover	873	Rudd	914
Rosw	841	Rovet	874	Ruddar	914
Rot	842	Rovi	875	Rude	915
Rote	843	Row	876	Rudi	916
Rotg	844	Rowan	877	Rudo	917
Roth	845	Rowe	878	Rudra	917
Rothen	846	Rowe, M.	879	Rue	918
Roths	847	Rowel	881	Ruef	919
Rothw	848	Rowi	882	Ruel	921
Rotr	849	Rowl	883	Ruf	922
Rott	851	Rowle	884	Ruffi	923
Rou	852	Rowman	884	Ruffn	924
Roub	853	Rows	885	Ruffo	925
Rouc	854	Rox	886	Rufi	926
Roug	855	Roxb	887	Rufu	927
Rouget	856	Roy	888	Rug	928
Roui	857	Royal	888	Rugg	929
Rouj	858	Roychoudhury	888	Ruggi	931
Roul	859	Roye	889	Ruggl	932
Roup	861	Royer	891	Ruh	933
Rouq	862	Royo	892	Ruhel	933
Rous	863	Roz	893	Rui	934
Rouss	864	Ru	894	Rul	935
Roussel	865	Ruben	895	Rum	936
Roussele	866	Rubi	896	Rumm	937
Rousset	867	Rubr	897	Rums	938
Roust	868	Ruc	898	Run	939
Rout	869	Ruch	899	Rund	941
Roux	871	Ruck	911	Rung	942
Rouy	872	Ruckers	912	Ruo	944
Rov	873	Rud	913	Rup	945

Rupp	946
Rupr	947
Rur	948
Rural	948
Rus	949
Rusch	951
Rush	952
Rush, M.	953
Rusht	954
Rushw	955
Rusk	956
Ruskin	956
Rusp	957
Russ	958
Russel	959
Russell	961
Russell, D.	962
Russell, F.	963
Russell, J.	964
Russell, M.	965
Russell, P.	966
Russell, S.	967
Russell, W.	968
Russi	969
Russia	969
Rust	971
Rustogi	971
Rustomji	971
Rut	972
Rutg	973
Ruth	974
Rutherf	975
Ruthv	976
Ruti	977
Rutl	978
Rutland, M.	979
Rutledge	981
Rutt	982
Ruv	983
Rux	984
Ruy	985
Ruyt	986
Ruz	987
Ry	988
Ryan	989
Ryan, M.	989
Ryc	991
Ryd	992
Rye	993
Ryl	994
Rym	995
Rys	996
Ryt	997
Ryv	998
Rz	999

S

Sa	111
Saadat	111
Saar	112
Saarc	112
Sab	113
Sabade	113
Sabar	113
Sabata	113
Sabb	114
Sabe	115
Sabharwal	114
Sabi	116
Sabir	116
Sabl	117
Saboo	117
Sabr	118
Sabrimala	118
Sac	119
Sach	121
Sachar	121
Sachdev	121
Sachdeva	121
Sachidananda	121
Sachs	121
Saco	122
Sacr	123
Sad	124
Sadat	124
Sade	125
Sadhak	125
Sadhale	125
Sadhu	125
Sadiq	125
Sadl	126
Sae	127
Saeed	127
Saf	128

Safaya	128
Safdar	128
Safi	128
Sag	129
Sagar	129
Saggar	129
Saghvi	225
Sagwan	226
Sah	131
Sah	131
Saha	131
Sahani	131
Saharaj	131
Sahay	131
Sahi	131
Sahir	131
Sahni	131
Sahoo	131
Sahu	131
Sai	132
Saidpur	132
Saigal	132
Saikia	132
Sain	132
Saini	132
Saint,A	133
Saint,An	134
Saint,B	135
Saint,C	136
Saint,D	137
Saint,E	137
Saint,F	138
Saint,G	139
Saint,H	141
Saint,I	142
Saint,J	143
Saint,Ju	144
Saint,L	145
Saint,M	146
Saint,N	147
Saint,O	148
Saint,P	149
Saint,R	151
Saint,S	152
Saint,Simon	153
Saint,U	154
Saint,V	155
Sainte	156
Sais	158
Saiut	158
Sajan	158
Sajay	158
Sajeev	158
Sajiva	158
Sajjan	158
Sakhuja	158
Saklani	158
Saksena	158
Sal	159
Salam	169
Salan	161
Salar	161
Sald	162
Sale	163
Salg	164
Sali	165
Salim	165
Salis	166
Salisbury	167
Sall	168
Sallo	169
Salm	171
Salman	171
Salmon	172
Salo	173
Salomon	174
Salon	175
Sals	175
Salt	176
Salter	177
Saltm	178
Salto	179
Salu	181
Saluja	181
Salv	182
Salve	183
Salvi	184
Salvin	185
Salvo	186
Salwi	186
Sam	187
Samaddar	187
Samaj	187

Samal	187
Samant	187
Samarth	187
Samba	187
Sambhi	187
Samh	188
Sami	188
Samiuddin	188
Samm	189
Samo	191
Samp	192
Sampat	192
Sampath	192
Sampooran	192
Sampurananda	192
Sams	193
Samuel	193
San,F	195
San,L	196
San,S	197
Sanajaola	197
Sanb	198
Sanborn	198
Sanc	199
Sanch	211
Sancr	212
Sand	213
Sande	214
Sandeep	214
Sanders	215
Sanderson	216
Sandf	217
Sandhu	217
Sandhya	217
Sando	218
Sandr	219
Sands	221
Sandy	222
Sane	223
Sanf	224
Sang	225
Sangal	225
Sangam	225
Sangat	225
Sangh	225
Sangm	225
Sangr	226
Sani	227
Sanjay	227
Sankalia	227
Sankar	227
Sankaracharya	227
Sankaram	227
Sankhdher	227
Sann	228
Sans	229
Sansar	229
Sanskrit	229
Sant	231
Santag	232
Santar	233
Sante	234
Santhanam	234
Santi	235
Santiago	235
Santiniketan	235
Santis	236
Santo	237
Santokh	237
Santosh	237
Sanu	238
Sanwal	238
Sanyal	238
Sao	239
Sap	241
Sapeh	241
Sapna	241
Sapru	241
Saq	242
Sar	243
Sarabhai	243
Sarad	243
Saradananda	243
Saraf	243
Saran	243
Sarangi	243
Saraswat	243
Sard	244
Sardar	244
Sardara	244
Sardesai	244
Sareen	244
Sarg	245

Sarin	245	Satu	254	Sayeed	274
Sarkar	245	Satvir	254	Sayer	274
Sarm	246	Satya	254	Sayl	275
Sarma	246	Satyajit	254	Sba	276
Saroj	246	Satyanarayan	254	Sca	277
Saroop	246	Satyindra	254	Scae	278
Sarr	247	Sau	255	Scal	279
Sars	248	Saul	256	Scalab	281
Sarsavati	243	Saun	257	Scali	282
Sart	249	Saup	258	Scam	283
Sarto	251	Saur	259	Scap	284
Saruk	251	Saut	261	Scar	285
Sarup	251	Sauv	262	Scarl	286
Sarwan	251	Sav	263	Scars	287
Sarwar	251	Savage, J.	264	Scav	288
Sas	252	Savar	265	Sce	289
Sasi	252	Savarkar	265	Sch	291
Sastri	252	Savas	266	Schad	292
Sat	253	Savi	267	Schae	293
Satapathy	253	Savo	268	Schaef	294
Satchidananda	253	Savot	269	Schaer	295
Sathe	253	Saw	271	Schaf	296
Sathyanarayana	253	Sawan	271	Schal	297
Sati	253	Sawant	271	Schall	298
Satija	253	Sawhney	271	Scham	299
Satinder	253	Sawyel	274	Schar	311
Satish	253	Sax	272	Schat	312
Satnam	253	Saxena	272	Schau	313
Satpal	253	Saxo	273	Schaum	299
Satpathi	253	Say	274	Sche	314
Sattar	253	Sayal	274	Sched	315

Schef	316
Scheffer, J.	317
Schei	318
Scheif	319
Scheit	321
Schel	322
Schem	323
Schen	324
Schep	325
Scher	326
Schet	327
Scheu	328
Schi	329
Schick	331
Schie	332
Schif	333
Schil	334
Schim	335
Schin	336
Schir	337
Schl	338
Schle	339
Schlei	341
Schles	342
Schleu	343
Schli	344
Schlo	345
Schlu	346
Schm	347
Schmi	348
Schmidt	349
Schmidt, F.	351
Schmidt, J.	352
Schmidt, L.	353
Schmidt, S.	354
Schmit	355
Schmo	356
Schn	357
Schne	358
Schneider, J.	359
Schni	361
Schno	362
Scho	363
Schoe	364
Schoen	365
Schoenl	366
Schoep	367
Schol	368
Schom	369
Schon	371
Schoo	372
School	372
Schop	373
Schor	374
Schot	375
Schou	376
Schra	377
Schrei	378
Schrey	379
Schro	381
Schroet	382
Schroff	382
Schu	383
Schube	384
Schue	385
Schul	386
Schulberg	368
Schultz	387
Schulz	388
Schulz, J.	389
Schulze	391
Schum	392
Schun	393
Schur	394
Schus	395
Schut	396
Schuy	397
Schw	398
Schwar	399
Schwarz	411
Schwe	412
Schwei	413
Schwell	414
Schwem	414
Schwer	415
Sci	416
Scin	417
Scip	418
Scir	419
Sco	421
Scog	422
Scor	423
Scot	424

Scott	425	Seetharam	453	Sep	479
Scott, G.	426	Seg	454	Sepharial	479
Scott, J.	427	Segr	455	Ser	481
Scott, M.	428	Segu	456	Seras	482
Scott, S.	429	Sehgal	456	Sere	483
Scott, W.	431	Sei	457	Serg	484
Scou	432	Seid	458	Seri	485
Scr	433	Seif	459	Serm	486
Scri	434	Seil	461	Sermon	486
Scro	435	Seis	462	Serr	487
Scu	436	Sej	463	Serre	488
Scul	437	Sekhar	463	Serro	489
Sea	438	Sekhon	463	Serv	491
Seal	438	Sel	464	Servin	492
Sear	439	Self	465	Ses	493
Seat	441	Selk	466	Sesadri	493
Seav	442	Sell	467	Sesagini	493
Seb	443	Sello	468	Seshadri	493
Sebastain	443	Selv	469	Seshagini	493
Sec	444	Sem	471	Sest	494
Seco	445	Semi	471	Set	495
Secr	446	Seml	472	Setaluad	495
Sed	447	Semp	473	Seth	495
Sedg	448	Sen	474	Sethi	495
Sedl	449	Senapati	474	Sethna	495
See	451	Sene	475	Setia	495
Seel	452	Senf	476	Seu	496
Seem	453	Sengar	476	Sev	497
Seema	453	Sengupta	476	Sever	498
Seetal	453	Seni	477	Severus	499
Seetha	453	Senn	478	Sevi	511

Sew	512
Sewa	512
Sewak	512
Sewall, S.	513
Seward	514
Sewel	515
Sewell	516
Sewell, S.	517
Sex	518
Sey	519
Seym	521
Seyt	522
Sfo	523
Sha	524
Shabbir	524
Shaf	525
Shafi	525
Shah	525
Shahane	525
Shahi	525
Shai	526
Shaida	526
Shaikh	526
Shak	527
Shakespeare	527
Shakuntla	527
Shal	528
Sham	528
Shamsher	528
Shamsuddin	528
Shan	528
Shangh	528
Shank	528
Shankar	528
Shankaracharya	528
Shanta	528
Shanti	528
Shap	529
Shapino	529
Shar	531
Shara	531
Sharad	531
Sharan	531
Sharda	531
Sharif	531
Sharimali	531
Sharma	531
Sharp	531
Sharpe	532
Shashi	532
Shastri	532
Shat	533
Shaw	534
Shaw, L.	535
Shaw, S.	536
Shaw, W.	537
Shay	538
She	539
Shed	541
Shef	542
Shei	543
Sheil	543
Shekhar	543
Shel	544
Shelley	545
Shen	546
Shenoy	546
Shep	547
Sheph	548
Shepp	549
Sher	551
Shergil	551
Sheri	552
Sherlekar	552
Sherm	553
Sherman	553
Sherw	554
Sherwani	554
Sheth	554
Shetty	554
Shi	555
Shil	556
Shilling	556
Shillong	556
Shimla	556
Shinde	556
Ship	557
Shir	558
Shirali	558
Shirur	558
Shisodia	558
Shiv	558
Shivani	558

Shivhare	558	Sidhu	568	Simon	594
Shiviah	558	Sidn	569	Simon, J.	595
Sho	559	Sie	571	Simon, P.	596
Shoal	559	Sien	572	Simond	597
Shobha	559	Sies	573	Simone	598
Shome	559	Sig	574	Simoni	599
Short	559	Sigf	575	Simons	611
Shourie	559	Sigi	576	Simp	612
Shr	561	Sigis	577	Simps	613
Shree	561	Sign	578	Simpson	613
Shreshtha	561	Sigu	579	Sims	614
Shri	561	Sikandar	579	Sin	615
Shriman	561	Sikdar	579	Sincl	616
Shrivastva	561	Sikh	579	Sindhu	616
Shu	562	Sikka	579	Sindhuwani	616
Shubh	562	Sikkim	579	Sing	617
Shukla	562	Sil	581	Singal	617
Shyam	562	Silb	582	Singapore	617
Sia	562	Silchar	582	Singer	617
Sib	563	Sili	583	Singh	617
Sibal	563	Sill	584	Singhal	617
Sibl	564	Silo	585	Singhvi	617
Sic	565	Silv	586	Singl	617
Sici	566	Silva	586	Sinha	617
Sico	567	Silve	587	Sins	618
Sid	568	Sim	588	Sir	619
Sidana	568	Sime	589	Siraj	619
Siddiqi	568	Simha	589	Sircar	619
Siddique	568	Siml	591	Siri	619
Sidh	568	Simm	592	Sirm	621
Sidharth	568	Simo	593	Sirsikar	621

Sis	622
Sism	623
Sisodia	623
Sister	623
Sistla	623
Sita	623
Sitaram	623
Siv	624
Siva	624
Sivananda	624
Sivaprasad	624
Sivaram	624
Sivaraman	624
Sivaswami	624
Six	625
Ska	626
Ske	627
Ski	628
Skinner	628
Skoda	629
Skr	629
Sla	631
Slater	631
Sle	632
Sli	633
Slo	634
Sma	635
Small	635
Smar	636
Smart	636
Sme	637
Smel	638
Smi	639
Smil	641
Smiragila	641
Smit	642
Smith	643
Smith, B.	643
Smith, C.	644
Smith, D.	645
Smith, E.	646
Smith, F.	647
Smith, G.	648
Smith, H.	649
Smith, J.	651
Smith, John	652
Smith, Jos.	653
Smith, L.	654
Smith, M.	655
Smith, O.	656
Smith, R.	657
Smith, Robert	658
Smith, S.	659
Smith, Sol	661
Smith, T.	662
Smith, W.	663
Smith, Wm.	664
Smits	665
Smo	666
Smy	667
Smythe	668
Sna	669
Sne	671
Sni	672
Sno	673
Snow	674
Snowden	674
Snoween	674
Sny	675
Soa	676
Sob	677
Sobti	677
Soc	678
Society	678
Sod	679
Soda	679
Sodhi	679
Soe	681
Sog	682
Sogani	682
Sohail	682
Sohan	682
Soi	683
Soil	683
Sol	684
Solanki	684
Solar	684
Sole	685
Soli	686
Solis	687
Soll	688
Solo	689
Solomon	689

Solt	691	Sous	725	Spil	756
Soly	692	Sout	726	Spin	757
Som	693	South	726	Spino	758
Somani	693	Southe	727	Spir	759
Somashekar	693	Southw	728	Spit	761
Somer	694	Souv	729	Spo	762
Somers	695	Sovvani	729	Spon	763
Somerv	696	Sow	731	Spoo	764
Somm	697	Spa	732	Spot	765
Son	698	Spaf	733	Spr	766
Sona	698	Spal	734	Spran	767
Sondhi	698	Span	735	Spre	768
Sone	698	Spar	736	Spri	769
Soni	698	Sparr	737	Spro	771
Sonn	699	Spat	738	Spu	772
Sonw	699	Spau	739	Squ	773
Soo	711	Spe	741	Squir	774
Sood	711	Spear	741	Sree	774
Sop	712	Spee	742	Sreenivasan	774
Sor	713	Spel	743	Sri	774
Sori	714	Spen	744	Srinath	774
Sos	715	Spencer	745	Srinivasa	774
Sost	716	Spencer, S.	746	Sriniwas	774
Sot	717	Spene	747	Sriram	774
Soto	718	Spens	748	Srivastan	774
Sou	719	Sper	749	Srivastava	774
Souf	721	Sperr	751	Srivatsan	774
Soul	722	Spet	752	Sta	775
Souli	723	Sph	753	Stad	776
Soum	724	Spi	754	Stadl	777
Soundara	724	Spie	755	Stae	778

Staf	779
Stah	781
Stai	782
Staley	782
Stalin	782
Stam	783
Stamp	783
Stan	784
Stand	785
Standing	785
Stanford	785
Stanh	786
Stanl	787
Stanley, J.	788
Stanley, S.	789
Stans	791
Stant	792
Stap	793
Stapl	794
Star	795
Stark	795
Starr	796
Stat	797
State	797
Statistical	797
Stau	798
Ste	799
Steb	811
Sted	812
Stee	813
Steel	813
Steele	814
Steev	815
Stef	816
Steffe	817
Stei	818
Stein	819
Steind	821
Steine	822
Steinm	823
Stel	824
Sten	825
Sten	825
Steno	826
Step	827
Stephen	828
Stephen, M.	829
Stephen, S.	831
Stephens	832
Stephens, G.	833
Stephens, L.	834
Stephens, R.	835
Stephenson	836
Stephenson, R.	837
Ster	838
Stern	839
Stet	841
Steu	842
Stev	843
Stevens	844
Stevens, M.	845
Stevens, S.	846
Stevenson	847
Stevenson, M.	848
Stew	849
Stewart, M.	851
Stewart, T.	852
Stey	853
Sti	854
Stie	855
Stig	855
Stil	856
Still	857
Stim	858
Stimp	859
Stir	861
Stit	862
Sto	863
Stob	863
Stoc	864
Stockl	865
Stockt	866
Stod	867
Stoddard, M.	868
Stoddard, S.	869
Stoe	871
Stoel	872
Stof	873
Stok	874
Stol	875
Stolt	876
Ston	877
Stone, J.	878

Stone, M.	879	Strol	921	Sudarsana	943
Stone, T.	881	Stron	922	Sudha	943
Stoo	882	Strong	923	Sudhakar	943
Stop	883	Strong, J	924	Sudhin	943
Stor	884	Strong,P	924	Sudi	943
Stork	885	Strot	925	Sue	944
Storr	886	Stroz	926	Suev	945
Story	887	Stru	927	Suf	946
Story, S.	888	Stry	928	Sug	947
Stou	889	Stu	929	Suhail	947
Stow	891	Stuart	931	Sui	948
Stowe	892	Stuart, J.	931	Sujan	948
Stowell	893	Stuart, M.	932	Sukhbir	948
Stra	894	Stud	933	Sukhwant	948
Strad	895	Student	933	Sul	949
Straf	896	Stuk	934	Sullivan, M.	951
Straf,P	925	Stur	935	Sullivan, S.	952
Stran	897	Sturm	936	Sully	953
Strat	898	Stut	937	Sulp	954
Strath	899	Stuy	938	Sultan	954
Stratt	911	Sua	939	Sum	955
Strau	912	Sub	941	Suman	955
Straw	913	Subba	941	Summer	955
Stre	914	Suber	941	Sumn	956
Stree	914	Subh	941	Sun	957
Street	915	Subhas	941	Sundarajan	957
Stri	916	Subramaniam	941	Sundaram	957
Strickl	917	Subramanyam	941	Sundaresan	957
Strin	918	Suc	942	Sunder	957
Stro	919	Sucheta	941	Sunderl	958
Strog	921	Sud	943	Sundharam	958

Suneja	958
Sunita	958
Sup	959
Supe	959
Supreme	959
Sur	961
Sur	961
Suraj	961
Suratkar	961
Surdas	961
Suresh	961
Suri	961
Surinder	961
Surjeet	961
Surjit	961
Surr	962
Surv	963
Suryarao	963
Suryavanshi	963
Sus	964
Susheel	964
Sushil	964
Suss	964
Sut	965
Suth	966
Sutt	967
Sutton	967
Suz	968
Svi	969
Swa	971
Swain	971
Swami	971
Swaminathan	971
Swamy	971
Swan	972
Swapna	972
Swar	973
Swaran	973
Swaroop	973
Swarup	973
Swe	974
Sweden	974
Swet	975
Swi	976
Swift	977
Swin	978
Swint	979
Sya	981
Syal	981
Syamala	981
Syd	982
Syed	982
Syk	983
Sykes	983
Syl	984
Sylv	985
Sym	986
Symm	987
Symo	988
Symp	989
Syms	991
Syn	992
Syng	993
Syp	994
Syr	995
Sza	996
Sze	997
Szi	998
Szy	999

T

Ta	111
Tab	112
Tabassum	112
Tabe	113
Tabo	114
Tac	115
Tacf	116
Tach	117
Taci	118
Tack	118
Taco	119
Tad	121
Tadas	121
Tado	122
Tae	123
Taf	124
Tag	125
Tagare	125
Tagl	126
Taglias	127
Taglio	128
Tagore	128
Taher	128

Name	Number
Tahir	128
Tahtinen	128
Tai	129
Tail	131
Taille	132
Tailli	133
Taimini	133
Taimni	133
Tain	134
Tais	135
Taiwan	133
Tak	136
Takle	136
Tal	137
Talbot	138
Talbot, G.	139
Talbot, M.	141
Talbot, S.	142
Tale	143
Talf	144
Talh	145
Tali	146
Talib	146
Talk	146
Tall	147
Talley	148
Talli	149
Talm	151
Talo	152
Talukdar	152
Talwar	152
Tam	153
Tamaskar	153
Tamb	154
Tambe	155
Tambou	156
Tame	157
Tami	158
Tamilnadu	158
Tamp	159
Tan	161
Tanaka	161
Tanc	162
Tand	163
Tane	164
Taneja	164
Tank	165
Tann	166
Tanner, M.	167
Tans	168
Tant	169
Tanvi	169
Tanwar	169
Tanz	171
Tao	171
Taori	171
Tap	172
Tapan	172
Tapl	173
Tapp	174
Tappan, M.	175
Tar	176
Tara	176
Taras	177
Tarau	178
Tarb	179
Tard	181
Tardieu	182
Tardif	183
Tare	184
Targ	185
Tari	186
Tarin	187
Tarkunde	187
Tarl	188
Tarlekar	188
Tarlok	188
Tarn	189
Taro	191
Tarr	192
Tars	193
Tartar	194
Tarti	195
Taru	196
Tas	197
Task	198
Tasm	199
Tass	211
Tasse	212
Tassi	213
Tasso	214
Tasson	215
Tat	216

Tata	216
Tate, M.	217
Tath	218
Tati	219
Tatt	221
Tau	222
Taubn	223
Tauc	224
Taul	225
Tauleen	225
Taun	226
Tauns	226
Taup	227
Taus	228
Taut	229
Tav	231
Tave	232
Taver	233
Taverni	234
Tavo	234
Tax	235
Taxman	235
Tay	236
Tayler	237
Taylor	238
Taylor, C.	239
Taylor, F.	241
Taylor, H.	242
Taylor, J.	243
Taylor, M.	244
Taylor, P.	245
Taylor, S.	246
Taylor, W.	247
Taz	248
Tc	249
Tche	251
Tcho	252
Te	253
Teb	254
Tec	255
Ted	256
Tedm	257
Tee	258
Tef	259
Teg	261
Tei	262
Teif	263
Teil	264
Teis	265
Teix	266
Teja	266
Tejinder	266
Tejomurthy	266
Tejvir	266
Tejwani	266
Tel	267
Tele	267
Telem	268
Telengana	268
Teles	269
Telf	271
Teli	272
Tell	273
Teller	274
Tellez	275
Telli	276
Tello	277
Telu	277
Tem	278
Teme	279
Temm	281
Temp	282
Tempest, M.	283
Templ	284
Templar	284
Temple	285
Temple, G.	285
Temple, M.	286
Temple, S.	287
Templet	288
Ten	289
Tend	291
Tendon	291
Tendulkar	291
Tene	292
Teni	293
Tenis	294
Tenn	295
Tennant, M.	296
Tenne	297
Tenney	298
Tenney, M.	299
Tenni	311

Tennis	311	Testi	344	Tham	366
Tenny	312	Testo	345	Thampan	366
Tent	313	Testu	346	Than	367
Teo	314	Tet	347	Thandani	367
Ter	315	Tete	347	Thangaraj	367
Tere	316	Tetr	348	Thani	367
Terg	317	Tetz	349	Thankappan	367
Terh	318	Teu	351	Thapa	367
Term	319	Teut	352	Thapan	367
Tern	321	Tev	353	Thapar	367
Terp	322	Tew	261	Tharoor	367
Terr	323	Tew	354	Tharu	367
Terras	324	Tewari	354	Thau	368
Terre	325	Tex	355	Thay	369
Terri	326	Tey	356	Thayer, G.	371
Terrin	327	Tez	356	Thayer, M.	372
Terro	328	Th	357	Thayer, S.	373
Terry	329	Thac	358	The	374
Ters	331	Thacher, G.	359	Theb	375
Tert	332	Thacher, M.	361	Thei	376
Terw	333	Thacher, S.	362	Theim	377
Terz	334	Thack	363	Their	377
Tes	335	Thacker	363	Thek	378
Tesau	336	Thadani	363	Thel	379
Tesc	337	Thai	364	Thelo	381
Tesla	337	Thailand	365	Thelw	382
Tess	338	Thairani	364	Them	383
Tessi	339	Thakar	364	Then	384
Tessin	341	Thakkar	364	Thengadi	384
Test	342	Thakur	364	Theo	385
Teste	343	Thal	365	Theoc	386

Theod	387
Theodo	388
Theodore	388
Theodos	389
Theog	391
Theon	392
Theop	393
Theophi	394
Theopo	395
Theor	396
Theos	397
Theosophical	397
Ther	398
Theraja	398
Theri	399
Therm	411
Thero	412
Thes	413
Thess	414
Theu	415
Thev	416
Theveni	417
Theveno	418
Thew	419
Thex	421
Thi	422
Thiard	423
Thib	424
Thibaul	425
Thibaut	426
Thibo	427
Thic	428
Thie	429
Thiel	431
Thielm	432
Thiem	433
Thien	434
Thier	435
Thierry	436
Thierry, M.	437
Thiers	438
Thies	439
Thil	441
Thilo	442
Thim	443
Thio	444
Thir	445
Thirl	446
Thiro	447
Thiru	447
This	448
Tho	449
Thol	451
Thom	452
Thoman	453
Thomas	454
Thomas, C.	455
Thomas, F.	456
Thomas, H.	457
Thomas, J.	458
Thomas, M.	459
Thomas, P.	461
Thomas, S.	462
Thomas, W.	463
Thomass	464
Thomassy	465
Thomo	466
Thomp	467
Thompson	468
Thompson, C.	469
Thompson, F.	471
Thompson, H.	472
Thompson, J.	473
Thompson, M.	474
Thompson, P.	475
Thompson, S.	476
Thompson, T.	477
Thompson, W.	478
Thompton	478
Thoms	479
Thomsen	481
Thomson	482
Thomson, G.	483
Thomson, M.	484
Thomson, S.	485
Thomson, W.	486
Thor	487
Thorat	487
Thore	488
Thores	489
Thori	491
Thoris	492
Thork	493

Thorl	494	Thun	535	Tigl	567
Thorm	495	Thur	536	Tigr	568
Thorn	496	Thurl	537	Tigris	568
Thornb	497	Thurlo	538	Tikakar	568
Thornd	498	Thurm	539	Tike	568
Thorndi	499	Thurn	541	Tikku	568
Thorne	511	Thuro	542	Tikoo	568
Thorney	512	Thurs	543	Til	569
Thornt	513	Thurston	544	Tilak	569
Thornton, M.	514	Thurston, G.	545	Tild	571
Thornw	515	Thurston, M.	546	Tile	572
Thoro	516	Thurston, S.	547	Tili	573
Thorp	517	Thw	548	Till	574
Thorpe	518	Thy	549	Tille	575
Thorpe	518	Ti	551	Tillet	576
Thorpe, G.	519	Tib	552	Tilli	577
Thorpe, M.	521	Tibe	553	Tillo	578
Thorpe, S.	522	Tibn	554	Tilly	579
Thort	523	Tic	555	Tils	581
Thou	524	Tick	556	Tilwani	581
Thoui	525	Ticknor	557	Tim	582
Thour	526	Ticks	557	Timb	583
Thout	527	Tid	558	Time	583
Thouv	528	Tie	559	Timm	584
Thr	529	Tief	561	Timo	585
Thre	531	Tiel	562	Timp	586
Throat	487	Tiep	563	Tin	587
Thu	532	Tier	564	Tina	587
Thui	533	Tif	565	Tind	588
Thukral	533	Tig	566	Tink	589
Thul	534	Tiger	566	Tinn	591

Tins	592	Tk	626	Tomilson	659
Tint	593	To	627	Tomk	658
Tinu	593	Tob	628	Toml	659
Tio	594	Tobi	629	Tomm	661
Tip	595	Toc	631	Tomp	662
Tir	596	Tocq	632	Ton	663
Tirath	596	Tod	633	Tone	664
Tiri	597	Todd, G.	634	Tong	665
Tirkey	597	Todd, M.	635	Toni	664
Tirmiziz	597	Todd, S.	636	Tonk	665
Tiruvalluvar	597	Tode	637	Tonn	666
Tis	598	Todh	638	Tont	667
Tisch	599	Todl	639	Too	668
Tische	611	Toe	641	Toofan	668
Tischl	612	Toep	642	Tooke, M.	669
Tisd	613	Toes	643	Tool	671
Tisea	598	Tof	644	Toom	672
Tiss	614	Tog	645	Toor	672
Tissi	615	Toi	646	Top	673
Tisso	616	Tokhi	646	Tope	673
Tissot	616	Tol	647	Toph	674
Tit	617	Tolb	648	Topl	675
Titi	618	Tole	649	Tor	676
Titin	619	Toll	651	Torah	682
Tito	621	Tolm	652	Tord	677
Titt	622	Tolo	653	Tore	678
Titu	623	Tols	654	Toren	679
Tiwana	623	Tom	655	Tores	681
Tiwari	623	Tomar	655	Torg	682
Tix	624	Tomb	656	Tori	683
Tiz	625	Tomi	657	Torl	684

Torn	685	Tourn	728	Tracy, M.	762
Torno	686	Tourno	729	Trad	763
Torq	687	Touro	731	Trae	764
Torr	688	Tourr	732	Trag	765
Torre	689	Tourv	733	Trai	766
Torren	691	Tous	734	Traill, M.	767
Torrent	692	Tousse	735	Train	768
Torres	693	Tout	736	Tral	769
Torrey	694	Tow	737	Tram	771
Torri	695	Tower, M.	738	Tran	772
Torrig	696	Towers	739	Trap	773
Torrin	697	Towg	741	Trapp	774
Tors	698	Towl	742	Tras	775
Tort	699	Town	743	Trat	776
Torti	711	Towne	744	Trau	777
Torto	712	Townel	745	Trauts	778
Tos	713	Townl	746	Trav	779
Tose	714	Towns	747	Travers, M.	781
Toss	715	Townsend, G.	748	Travi	782
Tost	716	Townsend, M.	749	Trax	783
Tot	717	Townsend, S.	751	Tre	784
Toto	717	Townsend, W.	752	Trebo	785
Tott	718	Townsh	753	Tred	786
Totten	719	Townshend, M.	754	Trehan	786
Tottl	721	Townso	755	Trei	787
Tou	722	Toy	756	Trel	788
Toul	723	Toynbee	756	Trem	789
Toulm	724	Toz	757	Tremo	791
Toulo	725	Tr	758	Tren	792
Toup	726	Trac	759	Trench, M.	793
Tour	727	Tracy	761	Trenck	794

Trent	795
Tres	796
Tresh	797
Tresi	798
Tress	799
Treu	811
Trev	812
Trevi	813
Trevis	814
Trevo	815
Trevor, M.	816
Trew	817
Trez	818
Tri	819
Trian	821
Trib	822
Tribal	822
Tribhuvan	822
Tribune	822
Tric	823
Trico	824
Trident	824
Tridere	824
Trie	825
Trier	826
Tries	827
Trig	828
Trikha	828
Tril	829
Trim	831
Trimul	831
Trin	832
Trinci	833
Trio	834
Trip	835
Tripathi	835
Tripoli	835
Tripp	836
Tripura	836
Tris	837
Trist	838
Trit	839
Triv	841
Trivedi	841
Triveni	812
Trivn	842
Tro	843
Trog	844
Troi	845
Trol	846
Trollo	847
Trollope, M.	848
Trom	849
Tromp	851
Tron	852
Tronci	853
Trons	854
Troo	855
Trop	856
Tros	857
Trot	858
Trou	859
Troui	861
Trouv	862
Trow	863
Troy	864
Tru	865
Trud	866
Trum	867
Truman	867
Trumbull	868
Trumbull, J.	869
Trumbull, S.	871
Trump	871
Trur	872
Trus	873
Trut	874
Try	875
Tryp	876
Ts	877
Tscher	878
Tschi	879
Tschu	881
Tse	882
Tu	883
Tub	884
Tuber	885
Tuc	886
Tucci	886
Tuch	887
Tucher	888
Tuck	889
Tucker	891

Tucker, G.	892	Turb	931	Turv	963
Tucker, M.	893	Turc	932	Tus	964
Tucker, S.	894	Turco	933	Tuss	965
Tucker, W.	895	Ture	934	Tut	966
Tuckerman	896	Turen	935	Tutt	967
Tuckerman, M.	897	Turg	936	Tuy	968
Tucket	898	Turgo	937	Tw	969
Tud	899	Turi	938	Twain	969
Tudi	911	Turk	939	Twee	971
Tudo	912	Turl	941	Twenty	971
Tue	913	Turn	942	Twi	972
Tuesday	913	Turnbull	943	Twin	973
Tuf	914	Turnbull, M.	943	Twis	974
Tufts, M.	915	Turne	944	Twy	975
Tughlaq	915	Turner	945	Twys	976
Tuk	916	Turner, C.	945	Ty	977
Tul	917	Turner, F.	946	Tyabji	977
Tuli	917	Turner, H.	947	Tyagi	977
Tull	918	Turner, J.	948	Tyc	978
Tulloch	919	Turner, M.	949	Tye	979
Tulloch, M.	921	Turner, P.	951	Tyl	981
Tullus	922	Turner, S.	952	Tyler, G.	982
Tully	923	Turner, T.	953	Tyler, M.	983
Tulo	924	Turner, W.	954	Tyler, S.	984
Tum	925	Turnh	955	Tyler, W.	985
Tun	926	Turno	956	Tym	986
Tunda	926	Turp	957	Tyn	987
Tung	926	Turr	958	Tyndall	988
Tuns	927	Turrett	959	Tyng	989
Tup	928	Turri	961	Typ	991
Tur	929	Turt	962	Tyr	992

Tyrrell	993
Tys	994
Tyson	994
Tyt	995
Tytler	996
Tytler, S.	997
Tz	998
Tzs	999

U

Ua	11
Ub	12
Ube	13
Uber	14
Uberoi	14
Ubi	15
Uc	16
Uch	17
Ud	18
Ude	19
Udey	18
Udi	21
Ue	22
Uf	23
Uffi	24
Uffo	25
Ug	26
Uga	26
Ugar	26
Ugo	27
Ugr	27
Uh	28
Uhd	29
Uhl	31
Uht	32
Ui	33
Uk	34
Ukr	35
Ukraine	35
Ul	36
Ule	37
Ulf	38
Uli	39
Ull	41
Ulle	42
Ulm	43
Ulnich	45
Ulr	45
Uls	46
Ult	47
Um	48
Uma	48
Umapathy	48
Umar	48
Umbr	49
Umf	51
Uml	52
Umrao	52
Ums	53
Un	54
Una	54
Unani	54
Unde	55
Underw	56
UNESCO	56
Ung	57
Uni	58
Unicef	58
Union	58
United	58
University	58
Uniyal	58
Unni	58
Unny	58
Uno	58
Uns	59
Unt	61
Unw	62
Unz	63
Uo	64
Up	65
Upadhya	65
Upadhyay	65
Upadhyaya	65
Upas	65
Upd	66
Uph	67
Upm	68
Upnishads	65
Uppal	68
Upreti	68
Ups	69
Upt	71
Ur	72

Urbi	73
Urc	74
Ure	75
Uri	76
Url	77
Uro	78
Urq	79
Urr	81
Urs	82
Urv	83
Us	84
USA	84
Ush	85
Usha	85
Usl	86
Usman	86
Uss	87
USSR	87
Ust	88
Ut	89
Utl	91
Utpal	91
Utr	92
Utt	93
Uttam	93
Uttar	93
Uv	94
Uw	95
Ux	96
Uy	97
Uyt	98
Uz	99

V

Va	111
Vable	111
Vac	112
Vacc	113
Vaccar	114
Vacch	115
Vaccha	115
Vacchi	116
Vacco	117
Vach	118
Vachani	118
Vachaspati	118
Vacho	119
Vacq	121
Vad	122
Vadackumchery	122
Vade	123
Vadhvani	123
Vadi	124
Vadinaja	124
Vae	125
Vag	126
Vagale	126
Vagh	126
Vah	127
Vai	128
Vaid	128
Vaidya	128
Vaidyanathan	128
Vail	129
Vaill	131
Vais	132
Vaish	132
Vaishnav	132
Vaj	133
Vajpayi	133
Vak	134
Vakil	134
Val	135
Valad	136
Valar	137
Valaz	138
Valb	139
Valc	141
Valck	142
Valckenb	143
Vald	144
Valdes	145
Valdi	146
Valdo	147
Valdr	148
Vale	149
Valeg	151
Valen	152
Valens	153
Valent	154
Valenti	155
Valentin	156
Valentine	157
Valentine, J.	158

Valentine, P.	159	Vallot	193	Vanderh	233
Valentini	161	Vallou	194	Vanderho	234
Valer	162	Valls	195	Vanderl	235
Valeri	163	Valm	196	Vanderm	236
Valerio	164	Valmiki	196	Vanderme	237
Valeriu	165	Valmy	197	Vandermo	238
Valery	166	Valo	198	Vanderp	239
Vales	167	Valor	199	Vanders	241
Valet	168	Valp	211	Vanderw	242
Valg	169	Valpy	212	Vandeu	243
Valh	171	Valr	213	Vandev	244
Vali	172	Vals	214	Vandi	245
Valicha	172	Valt	215	Vando	246
Valin	173	Vam	216	Vandy	247
Valk	174	Van	217	Vandyk	248
Vall	175	Vanamali	217	Vane	249
Vallad	176	Vanb	218	Vane, M.	251
Vallan	177	Vanbr	219	Vanee	252
Vallar	178	Vanbu	221	Vang	253
Vallau	179	Vanc	222	Vanh	254
Valle	181	Vance	222	Vanhe	255
Vallee	182	Vanco	223	Vanho	256
Vallem	183	Vand	224	Vanhu	257
Valler	184	Vandana	224	Vani	258
Valles	185	Vande	225	Vanl	259
Vallet	186	Vandel	226	Vanloo	261
Vallett	187	Vanden	227	Vanm	262
Valli	188	Vander	228	Vanmo	263
Vallis	189	Vanderbu	229	Vann	264
Vallo	191	Vanderc	231	Vanne	265
Vallon	192	Vanderd	232	Vannes	266

Vannet	267	Varenn	295	Vasco	331
Vanni	268	Vares	296	Vase	332
Vannin	269	Varg	297	Vash	333
Vannu	271	Varghese	297	Vashisht	333
Vano	272	Vargu	298	Vasi	334
Vanp	273	Vari	299	Vasq	335
Vanr	274	Varil	311	Vass	336
Vanro	275	Varin	312	Vassall	337
Vans	276	Variu	313	Vasse	338
Vansa	277	Varl	314	Vassi	339
Vansc	278	Varley	315	Vast	341
Vansh	277	Varlo	316	Vasudev	341
Vansi	279	Varma	316	Vaswani	341
Vansp	281	Varman	316	Vat	342
Vant	282	Varn	317	Vater	343
Vanu	283	Varney	318	Vath	344
Vanv	284	Varnh	319	Vati	345
Vanw	285	Varni	321	Vatin	346
Vap	286	Varnu	322	Vatk	347
Var	287	Varo	323	Vato	348
Varadarajan	287	Varot	324	Vatr	349
Varalakshmi	287	Varr	325	Vats	349
Varan	288	Varshney	325	Vatsyayan	349
Varanasi	288	Vart	326	Vatt	351
Varc	289	Vart	621	Vatti	352
Vard	291	Varu	327	Vatuk	351
Vardak	291	Varun	327	Vau	353
Vardharajan	291	Vas	328	Vauban	354
Vare	292	Vasan	328	Vaubl	355
Varel	293	Vasanta	328	Vauc	356
Varen	294	Vasc	329	Vauch	357

Vaud	358
Vaudoy	359
Vaudr	361
Vaudrey	362
Vaug	363
Vaughan	364
Vaughan, C.	365
Vaughan, G.	366
Vaughan, J.	367
Vaughan, M.	368
Vaughan, S.	369
Vaughan, W.	371
Vaugi	372
Vaugo	373
Vaul	374
Vaulo	375
Vault	376
Vaum	377
Vauq	378
Vaus	379
Vaut	381
Vauv	382
Vauvi	383
Vaux	384
Vaux, G.	385
Vaux, M.	386
Vauxc	387
Vauz	388
Vav	389
Vavi	391
Vay	392
Vaz	393
Ve	394
Veau	395
Vec	396
Vecchi	397
Vecchio	398
Vece	399
Vecellio	411
Vecn	412
Veco	413
Ved	414
Vedant	414
Vedd	415
Vedekar	415
Vedeyar	415
Vedic	415
Vedo	416
Vee	417
Veen	418
Veena	418
Veer	419
Veerappan	419
Vees	421
Veg	422
Vegi	423
Vegl	424
Veh	425
Vei	426
Veil	427
Veit	428
Veitch	429
Veith	431
Vel	432
Velas	433
Velasq	434
Veld	435
Vele	436
Veli	437
Vell	438
Velle	439
Vello	441
Vellu	442
Velly	443
Velp	444
Velt	445
Veltman	445
Veltr	446
Ven	447
Venan	448
Venc	449
Vences	451
Vend	452
Vendr	453
Vene	454
Veneg	455
Venel	456
Venet	457
Venez	458
Veni	459
Venin	461
Venkaliah	461
Venkat	461

Venkatachalam	461	Verdi	484	Vermil	526
Venkatachari	461	Verdig	485	Vermo	527
Venkatappaiah	461	Verdo	486	Vermoo	528
Venkataraman	461	Verdu	487	Vern	529
Venkataramanayya	461	Verdy	488	Verne	531
Venkatarao	461	Vere	489	Vernet	532
Venkatareddy	461	Verel	491	Verneu	533
Venkataswara	461	Verels	492	Verney	534
Venn	462	Verg	493	Verney, M.	535
Venner	463	Vergar	494	Verni	536
Venni	464	Verge	495	Vernin	537
Vent	465	Verger	496	Verniz	538
Vento	466	Verghese	496	Verno	539
Ventr	467	Vergi	497	Vernon, G.	541
Ventu	468	Vergn	498	Vernon, M.	542
Venturi	469	Vergy	499	Vernon, S.	543
Venu	471	Verh	511	Vernu	544
Venugopal	471	Verhag	512	Verny	545
Venut	472	Verhe	513	Vero	546
Vepa	472	Verho	514	Veron	547
Ver	473	Verhu	515	Verona	548
Verac	474	Veri	516	Verone	549
Veral	475	Verin	517	Verp	551
Verap	475	Verj	518	Verpo	552
Verar	476	Verk	519	Verr	553
Verb	477	Verl	521	Verri	554
Verbi	478	Verm	522	Verril	555
Verbo	479	Verma	522	Verrim	556
Verc	481	Verme	523	Verrio	557
Verci	482	Vermeu	524	Verro	558
Verd	483	Vermi	525	Verru	559

Vers	561
Verschu	562
Verse	563
Verso	564
Verst	565
Versto	566
Vert	567
Verto	568
Veru	569
Verv	571
Verw	572
Very	573
Verz	574
Ves	575
Vesey	576
Vesi	577
Vesl	578
Vesp	579
Vespa	579
Vespu	581
Vesq	582
Vest	583
Vestr	584
Vet	585
Vetch	586
Veth	587
Veti	588
Vetr	589
Vett	591
Vetto	592
Vetu	593
Veu	594
Vey	595
Veys	596
Vez	597
Vi	598
Vial	599
Viale	611
Viall	612
Vialo	613
Vian	614
Vianen	615
Viani	616
Viann	617
Viar	618
Viardo	619
Vias	622
Viau	623
Vib	624
Vibi	625
Vibn	626
Vic	627
Vicar	628
Vicars	629
Vicat	631
Vice	632
Vicenti	633
Vich	634
Vici	635
Vick	636
Vickers	637
Vickery	637
Vicky	637
Vico	638
Vicom	639
Vicq	641
Vict	642
Victor	643
Victor, G.	643
Victor, M.	644
Victor, S.	645
Victorin	646
Vicu	647
Vid	648
Vidal, M.	649
Vidarbha	649
Vidau	651
Vide	652
Vidi	653
Vido	654
Vidu	655
Vidya	655
Vidyarthi	655
Vie	656
Viei	657
Vieillo	658
Viel	659
Viell	661
Vien	662
Vienne	663
Vienno	664
Vier	665
Viet	666

Vieu	667	Vilain	696	Villeq	741
Vieus	668	Vilar	697	Viller	742
Vieuv	669	Vilat	698	Villerm	743
Vieux	671	Vilb	699	Villero	744
Vig	672	Vilh	711	Villers	745
Vige	673	Vill	712	Villers, M.	746
Viger	674	Villaf	713	Villes	747
Vigh	675	Villal	714	Villet	748
Vigi	676	Villam	715	Villeu	749
Vigil	677	Villan	716	Villi	751
Vign	678	Villano	717	Villiers	752
Vignal	679	Villanu	718	Villiers, F.	753
Vignau	681	Villar	719	Villiers, J.	754
Vigne	682	Villaret	721	Villiers, M.	755
Vigner	683	Villari	722	Villiers, S.	756
Vignes	684	Villars	723	Villiers, W.	757
Vigni	685	Villars, G.	724	Villo	758
Vigno	686	Villars, M.	725	Villon	759
Vignon	687	Villars, S.	726	Villot	761
Vigny	688	Villav	727	Vilm	762
Vigo	689	Ville	728	Vils	763
Vigor	691	Villec	729	Vim	764
Vigr	692	Villef	731	Vimal	764
Vigu	693	Villeg	732	Vimo	765
Vigui	694	Villego	733	Vin	766
Vij	694	Villeh	734	Vinay	766
Vijay	694	Villel	735	Vinc	767
Vijayalakshmi	694	Villem	736	Vincent	768
Vikas	694	Villen	737	Vincent, C.	769
Vikram	694	Villene	738	Vincent, F.	771
Vil	695	Villep	739	Vincent, J.	772

Vincent, M.	773	Virey	815	Vitet	844
Vincent, S.	774	Virg	816	Vithal	844
Vincent, W.	775	Virgin	817	Vito	845
Vinch	776	Viri	818	Vitr	846
Vinci	777	Virk	818	Vitro	847
Vinck	778	Virl	819	Vitru	848
Vind	779	Virmani	819	Vitry	849
Vindi	781	Viru	821	Vitt	851
Vine	782	Vis	822	Vittal	851
Vinet	783	Visch	823	Vitti	852
Ving	784	Visco	824	Vitto	853
Vini	785	Visconti, G.	825	Vitu	854
Vink	786	Visconti, M.	826	Viv	855
Vinn	787	Visconti, S.	827	Vivari	856
Vino	788	Visd	828	Vive	857
Vinoba	788	Vise	829	Vivekananda	857
Vinod	788	Vishnu	829	Vivi	858
Vint	789	Vishva	829	Viviani	859
Vinton	791	Vishwanathan	829	Vivien	861
Vinton, G.	792	Visi	831	Vivier	862
Vinton, M.	793	Vism	832	Vivo	863
Vinton, S.	794	Viss	833	Viz	864
Vio	795	Visse	834	Vl	865
Violl	796	Vit	835	Vlam	866
Viom	797	Vital	836	Vlas	867
Vion	798	Vitalis	837	Vle	868
Viot	799	Vite	838	Vli	869
Vip	811	Vitel	839	Vliet	871
Vipo	812	Vitelli	841	Vo	872
Vir	813	Viten	842	Voelc	873
Vire	814	Viter	843	Voell	874

Voer	875	Volke	917	Voo	949
Voet	876	Volkh	918	Voor	951
Vog	877	Volkm	919	Vop	952
Vogel	878	Volko	921	Vor	953
Vogel, M.	879	Volky	922	Vora	953
Vogh	881	Voll	923	Voro	954
Vogi	882	Vollm	924	Vors	955
Vogl	883	Vollw	925	Vorster	956
Vogler, M.	884	Volm	926	Vort	957
Vogo	885	Voln	927	Vory	958
Vogt	886	Volney	928	Vos	959
Vogt, M.	887	Volo	929	Vose	961
Vogu	888	Volp	931	Vose, D.	962
Vohra	888	Volpi	932	Vose, H.	963
Voi	889	Volpin	933	Vose, J.	964
Voice	889	Vols	934	Vose, M.	965
Voigt	891	Volt	935	Vose, S.	966
Voigt, G.	892	Voltaire	935	Vose, W.	967
Voigt, M.	893	Voltch	936	Vosm	968
Voigt, S.	894	Volte	937	Voss	969
Voil	895	Volto	938	Vossi	971
Voir	896	Voltr	939	Vou	972
Vois	897	Voltu	941	Voul	973
Voit	898	Voltz	942	Vow	974
Vol	899	Volu	943	Voy	975
Volc	911	Volv	944	Voys	976
Volck	912	Volvo	944	Voz	977
Volckm	913	Von	945	Vr	978
Vold	914	Vond	946	Vre	979
Volg	915	Vonk	947	Vri	981
Volk	916	Vono	948	Vries	982

Vril	983
Vro	984
Vs	985
Vu	986
Vui	987
Vuil	988
Vuit	989
Vul	991
Vulp	992
Vuls	993
Vuo	994
Vuy	995
Vy	996
Vyas	996
Vyjanti	996
Vyr	997
Vys	998
Vz	999

W

Wa	111
Waas	112
Wac	113
Wachs	114
Wack	115
Wad	116
Waddell	116
Waddi	117
Waddington	118
Wade	119
Wade, M.	121
Wadekar	121
Wadh	122
Wadhera	122
Wadhwa	122
Wadhwani	122
Wadia	122
Wadl	123
Wads	124
Wadsworth	125
Wae	126
Wael	127
Waf	128
Wag	129
Wagen	131
Wagh	131
Wagle	131
Wagn	132
Wagner, G.	133
Wagner, M.	134
Wagner, S.	135
Wah	136
Wahlen	137
Wai	138
Waill	139
Wain	141
Wainwright	142
Wais	143
Wait	144
Waite	145
Wajid	145
Wak	146
Wake	146
Wakef	147
Wakeh	148
Wakel	149
Wal	151
Walch	152
Walch, J.	153
Walch, P.	154
Walck	155
Walco	156
Wald	157
Walde	158
Waldeg	159
Waldem	161
Walden	162
Walder	163
Waldm	164
Waldo	165
Waldor	166
Waldr	167
Walds	168
Wale	169
Walei	171
Wales	172
Wales, M.	173
Waley	173
Walf	174
Walg	175
Wali	176
Walia	176
Walk	177
Walker	178

Walker, D.	178
Walker, F.	179
Walker, J.	181
Walker, M.	182
Walker, P.	183
Walker, S.	184
Walker, T.	185
Walker, W.	186
Walkhlu	186
Wall	187
Wallace	187
Wallace, D.	188
Wallace, F.	189
Wallace, J.	191
Wallace, M.	192
Wallace, P.	193
Wallace, S.	194
Wallace, W.	195
Wallc	196
Wallen	197
Waller	198
Walley	199
Walli	211
Wallingf	212
Wallingt	213
Wallis	214
Wallo	215
Walm	216
Waln	217
Walp	218
Walpole, M.	219
Walr	221
Wals	222
Walsh	223
Walsh, D.	224
Walsh, J.	225
Walsh, M.	226
Walsh, S.	227
Walsh, W.	228
Walsi	229
Walt	231
Waltens	232
Walter, G.	232
Walter, M.	233
Walter, S.	234
Walters	235
Walth	236
Walther	237
Walto	238
Walton, G.	239
Walton, M.	241
Walw	242
Wam	243
Wan	244
Wand	245
Wang	246
Wanh	247
Wani	247
Wanl	248
Wann	249
Wans	251
Wap	252
War	253
Warburton	254
Warburton, M.	255
Ward	256
Ward, C.	257
Ward, F.	258
Ward, J.	259
Ward, M.	261
Ward, P.	262
Ward, S.	263
Ward, W.	264
Warde	265
Wardl	266
Ware	267
Ware, D.	268
Ware, J.	269
Ware, M.	271
Ware, S.	272
Ware, W.	273
Waren	274
Warh	275
Wari	276
Waring, M.	277
Warn	278
Warner	279
Warner, D.	281
Warner, J.	282
Warner, M.	283
Warner, S.	284
Warner, W.	285
Warr	286

Warren, C.	287
Warren, F.	288
Warren, J.	289
Warren, M.	291
Warren, P.	292
Warren, S.	293
Warren, W.	294
Warri	295
Wart	296
Wartens	297
Warto	298
Warw	299
Warwick, M.	311
Waryam	311
Was	312
Waser	313
Wash	314
Washburn, M.	315
Washi	316
Washington	317
Washington, G.	318
Washington, M.	319
Wass	321
Wasser	322
Wassi	323
Waswani	323
Waswaran	323
Wat	324
Waterf	325
Waterh	326
Waterl	327
Waterm	328
Waters	329
Waters, M.	331
Waterst	332
Waterw	333
Watk	334
Watke	335
Watkinson	336
Wats	337
Watson	337
Watson, D.	338
Watson, J.	339
Watson, M.	341
Watson, S.	342
Watson, W.	343
Watt	344
Watt, J.	345
Watt, P.	346
Watt,i	347
Watts	348
Watts, D.	349
Watts, J.	351
Watts, M.	352
Watts, S.	353
Wau	354
Waut	355
Wavell	355
Waw	356
Way	357
Wayl	358
Wayman	358
Wayn	359
Wazir	359
We	361
Weal	362
Weav	363
Web	364
Webb	365
Webb, G.	366
Webb, M.	367
Webb, S.	368
Webbe	369
Webber	371
Webber, M.	372
Weber	373
Weber, G.	374
Weber, M.	375
Weber, S.	376
Webs	377
Webster, C.	378
Webster, F.	379
Webster, J.	381
Webster, M.	382
Webster, P.	383
Webster, S.	384
Webster, W.	385
Wech	386
Weck	387
Wed	388
Wede	389
Wedel	391
Wedg	392

Wedgw	393	Weitz	436	Wendl	471
Wee	394	Wek	437	Wendo	472
Weeks	395	Wel	438	Wendt	473
Weeks, M.	396	Welch	439	Weng	474
Weem	397	Welch, M.	441	Weni	475
Weer	398	Welck	442	Wenl	476
Weev	399	Weld	443	Went	477
Weg	411	Weld, M.	444	Wentworth, G.	478
Wegn	412	Welde	445	Wentworth, M.	479
Weh	413	Welh	446	Wentz	481
Wehr	414	Well	447	Wenz	482
Wei	415	Weller	448	Wep	483
Weich	416	Welles	449	Wer	484
Weid	417	Wellesl	451	Werde	485
Weidm	418	Welli	452	Were	486
Weig	419	Wells	453	Weren	487
Weik	421	Wells, G.	454	Werf	488
Weil	422	Wells, M.	455	Werl	489
Wein	423	Wells, S.	456	Wern	491
Weiner	423	Wellw	457	Werner	492
Weinm	424	Wels	458	Werner, G.	493
Weir	425	Welse	459	Werner, M.	494
Weis	426	Welsh	461	Wernh	495
Weise	427	Welsh, J.	462	Werni	496
Weisk	428	Welsh, P.	463	Werns	497
Weiss	429	Welt	464	Werp	498
Weiss, J.	431	Welw	465	Wert	499
Weiss, P.	432	Wem	466	Wes	511
Weissen	433	Wen	467	Wesen	512
Weit	434	Wenc	468	Wesl	513
Weits	435	Wend	469	Wesley, M.	514

Wess	515
West	516
West, D.	517
West, J.	518
West, M.	519
West, S.	521
West, W.	522
Westb	523
Westc	524
Weste	525
Wester	526
Westerm	527
Westg	528
Westh	529
Westm	531
Westmi	532
Westmo	533
Westo	534
Weston, G.	535
Weston, P.	536
Westp	537
Westr	538
Wet	539
Wetm	541
Wett	542
Wetts	543
Wetz	544
Wex	545
Wey	546
Weye	547
Weyl	548
Weym	549
Wh	551
Whal	552
Whart	553
Wharton, M.	554
What	555
Whe	556
Wheatl	557
Wheato	558
Whed	559
Whee	561
Wheeler	562
Wheeler, G.	563
Wheeler, P.	564
Wheelo	565
Wheelw	566
Whelp	567
Whet	568
Whew	569
Whi	571
Whid	572
Whip	573
Whipple, J.	574
Whipple, P.	575
Whis	576
Whit	577
Whitaker, M.	578
Whitb	579
Whitc	581
White	582
White, C.	583
White, F.	584
White, J.	585
White, M.	586
White, P.	587
White, S.	588
White, W.	589
Whitef	591
Whiteh	592
Whiteho	593
Whitel	594
Whitf	595
Whitg	596
Whiti	597
Whiting	598
Whiting, G.	599
Whiting, M.	611
Whiting, S.	612
Whiting, W.	613
Whitm	614
Whitman	615
Whitman, M.	615
Whitmore	616
Whitney	617
Whitney, D.	618
Whitney, J.	619
Whitney, M.	621
Whitney, S.	622
Whitney, W.	623
Whitt	624
Whitti	625
Whitting	626

Whittl	627
Whitw	628
Who	628
Why	629
Wi	631
Wib	632
Wic	633
Wichi	634
Wichm	635
Wichn	636
Wick	637
Wickh	637
Wid	638
Wide	639
Widm	641
Wie	642
Wiede	643
Wiedem	644
Wieg	645
Wiel	646
Wien	647
Wier	648
Wies	649
Wiese	651
Wiess	652
Wif	653
Wig	654
Wigg	655
Wiggl	656
Wigh	657
Wightm	658
Wigm	659
Wign	661
Wigr	662
Wik	663
Wil	664
Wilbr	665
Wilbu	666
Wilc	667
Wild	668
Wildb	669
Wilde	671
Wilde, M.	672
Wilde,O	671
Wilder	673
Wildm	674
Wildt	675
Wile	676
Wilf	677
Wilh	678
Wili	679
Wilk	681
Wilkes	682
Wilki	683
Wilkins	684
Wilkins, M.	685
Wilkinson	686
Wilkinson, M.	687
Wilks	688
Will	689
Willar	691
Willard, D.	692
Willard, J.	693
Willard, M.	694
Willard, S.	695
Willard, W.	696
Willc	697
Wille	698
Willem	698
Willen	699
Willer	699
Willes	699
Willey	699
Willi	715
William	716
William, G.	717
William, M.	718
William, S.	719
Williams	721
Williams, C.	722
Williams, F.	723
Williams, J.	724
Williams, M.	725
Williams, P.	726
Williams, S.	727
Williams, W.	728
Williamson	729
Williamson, J.	731
Williamson, P.	732
Willin	733
Willis	734
Willis, M.	735

Willist	736	Wing	769	Wise	812
Willm	737	Wingf	771	Wise, M.	813
Willmo	738	Wingo	771	Wisem	814
Willo	739	Wingr	772	Wisn	815
Wills	741	Wink	773	Wiss	816
Willso	742	Winkelm	774	Wist	817
Wilm	743	Winkl	775	Wisw	818
Wilmo	744	Winn	776	Wit	819
Wilr	745	Wins	777	Wite	821
Wils	746	Winslow	778	With	822
Wilson, C.	747	Winslow, G.	779	Witheri	823
Wilson, F.	748	Winslow, M.	781	Withers	824
Wilson, J.	749	Winslow, S.	782	Witi	825
Wilson, M.	751	Winst	783	Wits	826
Wilson, P.	752	Winston	783	Witt	827
Wilson, S.	753	Wint	784	Witte	828
Wilson, W.	754	Winter, G.	785	Witten	829
Wilt	755	Winter, M.	786	Wittg	831
Wilton, M.	756	Winter, S.	787	Witti	832
Wim	757	Winterf	788	Witz	833
Win	758	Winth	789	Witzl	834
Winche	759	Winthrop	791	Wix	835
Winck	761	Winthrop, J.	792	Wl	836
Winckl	762	Winthrop, P.	793	Wo	837
Wind	763	Wintr	794	Wod	838
Windh	764	Winw	795	Wodes	839
Windi	765	Wio	796	Woe	841
Windows	765	Wip	797	Woel	842
Winds	766	Wir	798	Woer	843
Wine	767	Wirt	799	Wof	844
Wines	768	Wis	811	Wog	845

Woi	847
Wol	848
Wolcott	849
Wolcott, M.	851
Wold	852
Wolf	853
Wolf, J.	854
Wolf, P.	855
Wolffe	856
Wolffe, J.	857
Wolffe, P.	858
Wolfg	859
Wolfr	861
Wolk	862
Woll	863
Wolle	864
Wolm	865
Wolo	866
Wols	867
Wolt	868
Woltm	869
Wolz	871
Wom	872
Woo	873
Wood	874
Wood, C.	874
Wood, F.	875
Wood, J.	876
Wood, M.	877
Wood, P.	878
Wood, S.	879
Wood, W.	881
Woodbri	882
Woodbridge, M.	883
Woodbu	884
Woodbury, M.	885
Woodc	886
Woodf	887
Woodh	888
Woodho	889
Woodhu	891
Woodm	892
Woodr	893
Woods	894
Woods, J.	895
Woods, M.	896
Woods, S.	897
Woods, W.	898
Woodw	899
Woodward, J.	911
Woodward, P.	912
Wool	913
Woolm	914
Woolr	915
Wools	916
Woolw	917
Woot	918
Wor	919
Worcester, G.	921
Worcester, M.	922
Worcester, S.	923
Word	924
Wordsw	925
Wordsworth	925
Work	925
Workshop	925
Worl	926
World	926
Worm	927
Worm	928
Woro	929
Wors	931
Wort	932
Worth	933
Worthington	934
Worthington, M.	934
Wortl	935
Wot	936
Wott	937
Wou	938
Wr	939
Wran	941
Wrat	942
Wrax	943
Wre	944
Wren	945
Wri	946
Wright	947
Wright, F.	948
Wright, M.	952
Wright, S.	953
Wright, W.	954
Wright,G	949

Wright,J	951
Wris	955
Writ	956
Wro	957
Wroth	958
Wu	959
Wul	961
Wulfh	962
Wulfr	963
Wulfs	964
Wun	965
Wuns	966
Wur	967
Wurm	968
Wurt	969
Wurtz	971
Wurz	972
Wus	973
Wy	974
Wyatt	975
Wyatt, M.	976
Wyc	977
Wyd	978
Wye	979
Wyk	981
Wyl	982
Wyle	983
Wym	984
Wyn	985
Wynf	986
Wyng	987
Wynn	988
Wynne, M.	989
Wynt	991
Wyo	992
Wyr	993
Wys	994
Wyss	995
Wyt	996
Wytt	997
Wyv	998
Wz	999

X

Xa	1
Xan	2
Xav	3
Xavier	3
Xe	4
Xen	5
Xer	6
Xi	6
Xl	7
Xn	8
Xy	9

Y

Ya	11
Yac	12
Yadagiri	12
Yadav	12
Yagnik	12
Yah	13
Yaha	13
Yahoo	13
Yai	14
Yak	15
Yakesh	15
Yal	16
Yale	17
Yale, M.	18
Yales	19
Yan	21
Yane	22
Yani	23
Yann	24
Yanya	24
Yao	25
Yar	26
Yard	27
Yarf	28
Yarr	29
Yaseen	29
Yashpal	29
Yat	31
Yates, G.	32
Yates, M.	33
Yates, S.	34
Yates,W	34
Yati	34
Yatishuranand	34
Yatm	35
Yazdani	35
Yb	36
Ye	37

Yeam	38
Year	39
Yearbook	39
Yeat	41
Yeb	42
Yef	43
Yem	44
Yen	45
Yeo	46
Yep	47
Yesudas	47
Yet	48
Yez	49
Yh	51
Yl	52
Yn	53
Yo	54
Yodhraj	54
Yog	54
Yogendra	54
Yogi	54
Yon	55
Yonge, G.	56
Yonge, M.	57
Yonge, S.	58
Yonge, W.	59
Yonus	59
Yor	61
York, J.	62
York, P.	63
Yorke	64
Yorke, M.	65
Yot	66
You	67
Yougal	67
Young	68
Young, C.	69
Young, G	71
Young, H	72
Young, J.	73
Young, M.	74
Young, P.	75
Young, S.	76
Young, T.	77
Young, W.	78
Younghusband	78
Youngm	79
Youngs	81
Yous	82
Youss	83
Yoyo	83
Yoz	84
Yp	85
Yps	86
Yr	87
Yri	88
Yrie	89
Ys	91
Ysen	92
Yss	93
Yu	94
Yugandhar	94
Yukat	94
Yule	95
Yung	95
Yunus	95
Yusuf	95
Yuval	95
Yuvraj	95
Yv	96
Yve	97
Yves	98
Yvo	99

Z

Za	11
Zab	12
Zabar	12
Zac	13
Zacco	14
Zach	15
Zachar	16
Zacharia	16
Zacu	17
Zafar	17
Zag	18
Zah	19
Zahir	19
Zai	21
Zaidi	21
Zail	21
Zakaria	21
Zaki	21
Zakir	21

Zakk	21	Zeif	46	Zin	77
Zal	22	Zein	66	Zink	78
Zam	23	Zeis	47	Zins	79
Zaman	23	Zeit	48	Zinta	79
Zambo	24	Zel	49	Zir	81
Zamo	25	Zell	51	Zirak	81
Zamp	26	Zello	52	Zit	82
Zan	27	Zelo	52	Zo	83
Zane	28	Zelt	53	Zoc	84
Zang	29	Zen	54	Zoe	85
Zani	31	Zeno	55	Zoh	85
Zann	32	Zent	56	Zok	85
Zano	33	Zep	57	Zol	86
Zant	34	Zer	58	Zon	87
Zap	35	Zes	59	Zon	89
Zar	36	Zet	61	Zoo	87
Zardare	36	Zeu	62	Zoological	87
Zargar	36	Zev	63	Zop	88
Zari	37	Zi	64	Zor	89
Zaro	38	Ziaul	64	Zot	89
Zau	39	Zie	65	Zou	91
Zav	39	Zieg	66	Zoya	91
Zbar	39	Zies	67	Zs	92
Ze	41	Zif	68	Zu	93
Zea	41	Zil	69	Zuc	94
Zec	42	Zim	71	Zuck	94
Zed	43	Zimmer	72	Zun	95
Zee	43	Zimmermann	73	Zur	96
Zeenat	43	Zimmermann, G.	74	Zutshi	96
Zeg	44	Zimmermann, M.	75	Zw	97
Zei	45	Zimmermann, S.	76	Zwi	98
				Zy	99